H.S. HAYDEN,
(Dr. H. Hayd
CHILD AND ADOLESCENT PSYCHIATRY
#107, 22190 - 48th Avenue
Langley, BC V3A 3N5
TEL:530-7646 • FAX:534-6192

A CHILD'S THERAPY:
HOUR BY HOUR

A CHILD'S THERAPY: HOUR BY HOUR

Mary R. Haworth, Ph.D.

International Universities Press, Inc.
Madison, Connecticut

Second Printing, 1996

Library of Congress Cataloging-in-Publication Data

Haworth, Mary Robbins.
    A child's therapy: hour by hour / Mary R. Haworth.
      p.   cm.
    Bibliography: p.
    Includes index.
    ISBN 0-8236-0838-7
    1. Child psychotherapy—Technique.   I. Title.
    [DNLM: 1. Child Psychiatry. 2. Psychotherapy—in infancy &
childhood. 3. Psychotherapy—methods.   WS 350.2 H397c]
RJ504.H378   1990
618.92'8914-dc20
DNLM/DLC
for Library of Congress   89-15374
                                                         CIP

Manufactured in the United States of America

Contents

Preface

This volume presents an extensive and intensive examination of a nine-year-old boy's progress through nine months of psychotherapy. It is intended as an instructional exercise for beginning child therapists. Although no two cases will ever be alike, study of the approaches used by other therapists can aid the novice in understanding the dynamics and process of therapy, as it unfolds, as well as what helps and what hinders that process.

The Introduction provides a brief overview of the development of psychoanalytic and psychotherapeutic techniques for the treatment of young children, starting with the earliest work of Melanie Klein and Anna Freud in the 1920s, to the current eclectic approaches, of which the author's is one example.

A brief theoretical discussion of the therapeutic process is presented in Chapter 1, as well as pertinent background information concerning the child and his family. Results of the psychological evaluation, made prior to the initiation of therapy, are discussed in terms of the specific tests that were administered (Rorschach, House-Tree-Person, and Thematic Apperception Test). The concluding portion of Chapter 1 presents speculations based on the family history and test material, problem areas to be explored, and the possible underlying dynamics that might be revealed in therapy.

Chapter 2 presents the process notes as recorded by the therapist immediately after each of the thirty-two sessions, along with her marginal notes and speculations as to the possible significance of various play sequences. The therapist's interim and final reports, as well as comments from the psychiatrist who was seeing the mother, are included in this section.

Chapter 3 traces the development of individual themes as they appeared and were subsequently worked through in the course of therapy. Some repetition is obviously involved in order to relate a particular theme to others also occurring in the session under scrutiny, due to the multidetermined aspects of symbolism and play activity in general. Every attempt has been made to avoid excessive redundancy while at the same time emphasizing the interdependence of the various themes. To a certain extent, the entire course of therapy can be traced in broad outline by following any one them.

Chapter 4 follows the sequence of sessions from the therapist's viewpoint, pointing out why she did or said certain things and their positive or negative results; the occurrence of play disruptions with their apparent cause and effect; and where she may have moved in too soon or when she overlooked an obvious opportunity for a meaningful interpretation. The relationship that developed between the child and his therapist is also examined in the context of transference or treatment alliance connotations.

The chief purpose in presenting this case is as an instructional device for individual study or use in group discussions for beginning therapists. There are obviously many other ways in which the case could have been handled; certain areas (such as ego enhancement) could have been emphasized exclusively; or issues relating to the psychosexual stages could have been given sole prominence. Activities only indirectly relating to the child's referral symptoms could have been ignored until more obviously broached by the boy. Many other comments and interpretations could have been made in response to the same material. The presentation offered here leaves room for the exploration of other viewpoints and for in-depth theoretical discussions in a training setting.

Appreciation is extended to Edward J. Sheridan, Jr., M.D., Thomas L. Walsh, M.D., and Delbert T. Goates, M.D., for offering helpful insights into the underlying psychodynamics of the case, suggestions for the organization and presentation of the material, and additional background and collaborative information. Recognition is also due Karyn Sultan for her creative and efficient handling of the technical aspects of preparing the manuscript for publication.

Mary R. Haworth, Ph.D.
Washington, DC

Introduction

Just as the course of psychotherapeutic treatment of a young child is a dynamic, ever-changing process, so too has been the history of the field over the past sixty to seventy years. The earliest approaches either followed strictly psychoanalytic procedures, borrowed from Freud's work with adult patients, or represented modifications and adaptations more suited to the child's needs and capacities. Subsequent, and current, practices have represented a variety of treatment modalities focused not only on the individual child but extending to the family, school, and community.

Historical Overview

From the 1920s to the mid-1950s, the modes of treatment for the individual child clustered around two opposite poles: on the psychoanalytic side were Melanie Klein's early work along strictly analytic lines and Anna Freud's modifications of classical techniques based on considerations of the child's developmental milestones and limited analytic potentials. Erik Erikson and Selma Fraiberg further elaborated and adapted psychoanalytic procedures to fit the child's stages and needs.

At the opposite extreme, and somewhat later in time, another group of therapists was advocating "relationship ther-

1

apy," with emphasis on the therapist–child interaction as a model for all of the child's relationships. From here it was hardly a quantum leap to the nondirective school, modeled on Carl Rogers's work and developed as "play therapy" by Virginia Axline and Clark Moustakas.

In the past twenty-five to thirty years a number of mixed approaches have developed coincident with a broadening of the base of disciplines involved in working with children, pressures of time, and financial constraints which negate long-term treatment commitments, and an increased focus, by the helping professions, on crisis management in a broadened community base. Consequently, many contemporary therapists seem to be sampling bits and pieces from all that has gone before under the rubric of *child psychotherapy, psychodynamic psychotherapy,* or *psychoanalytically oriented psychotherapy.*

Early Psychoanalytic Methods

Melanie Klein conducted her first child analysis in England in 1919. Basing her strictly psychoanalytic approach (1932) on Sigmund Freud's work with adults, she started from the premise that, theoretically, there need be no difference in technique if one assumed that the child's play and symbolism could stand in the place of the dreams and free associations of adult patients. The analyst could interpret all of the child's play actions, fantasies, and resistances as representations of preconscious and unconscious conflicts.

Klein believed that a transference neurosis (similar to that with adults) does occur with children. By direct interpretations, in depth, the child would reexperience toward the therapist those early impulses, oedipal conflicts, and guilt reactions that were experienced originally with the parents. Furthermore, play symbolism should be translated directly with reference to the instinctual drives without first interpreting the defenses against such drives. All sessions should contain some transference interpretations, starting with the initial session where the analyst must, of necessity, need to speculate as to the symbolic representations being enacted in the child's play.

Anna Freud, in Vienna, was developing her distinctive approach to psychoanalytic work with children at about the same time as Melanie Klein. She emphasized the role of the ego in defensive operations and pointed to the need to incorporate educative aspects into the analysis. Initially, Anna Freud (1922–1935) felt that, while a young child could experience transference reactions, a true transference neurosis could not develop since the parental objects were still very much a factor in the child's life. In her introduction to a 1974 reissue of the earlier work she altered this view, stressing the dual nature of the analyst's role when working with children: the analyst is seen as a new and real person separate from the parents while at the same time numerous transference phenomena appear as the child uses the analyst for reworking attitudes and impulses originally directed toward the parents. Nevertheless, she felt that the original conflicts and their libidinal ramifications are rarely transferred totally from the parents to the analyst. She also has pointed out (1965) that children in analysis will repeat, by regression, their object relations from all levels of development. Pregenital and preoedipal elements will appear in the transference situation and need to be interpreted before oedipal issues can be resolved.

Anna Freud's early work (1936) described the protective role of the defense mechanisms as a means of containing the id impulses. Since the same type of defense would be used against the affects derived from the impulses as against the impulses themselves, she recommended first analyzing the resistances of the ego and the transformations of the affects as a means of understanding the underlying impulses. While the interpretation of transference and resistance and the increased attention to ego functions were seen as the main elements in her analytic approach, she also discussed (1965) other aspects of the process that could be seen as unique to analytic work with children: namely, the use of verbalization and clarification to relieve anxiety; suggestions, which place the analyst in an educational role; and reassurance, which is an inevitable aspect of a close adult–child relationship.

Anna Freud (1965) emphasized the need for a sensitive understanding of the normal characteristics of growth and maturation. She developed the concept of developmental lines as a means of tracing and comparing the linear growth of various ego functions, the transitions through the libidinal phases, and the interactions between the two at each stage of development.

Erik Erikson clarified several concepts that have added a new dimension to the psychoanalytic literature. "Ego identity" was distinguished from identification as a unique realization of self (1959). He was the first to posit a climactic type of disorganization in a child's play which he labeled "play disruption" (1940). This phenomenon appears when repressed material comes to the surface; anxiety and guilt are heightened; all defenses have failed; and the play is abruptly immobilized. He stressed that at this point meaningful interpretations are necessary to relieve the anxiety and to facilitate insight.

Erikson has been especially interested in the ways children use toys in the playroom. One of his earliest papers (1940) emphasized the metaphoric and symbolic meanings of play as representations of conflicts. He suggested that children transfer their ambivalence toward the parents onto the therapist, while representing the conflict metaphorically in their play in the protective environment provided by a sympathetic adult. He has been very attuned to the interplay of social, verbal, spatial, and bodily forms of expression in children's play.

Erikson's "Eight Stages of Man" (1950) provided a new

framework for understanding the positive and negative potentials inherent in the child's psychosexual maturation via stage-specific periods throughout the life cycle from infancy through adulthood. His insightful summaries of the dynamic aspects of each stage serve as an aid in tracing ego functions, regressions, and fixations over time.

Selma Fraiberg's changing views on transference paralleled those of Anna Freud. In her early reports (1951) she pointed out that, while a child's neurosis might be transferred into the therapy situation, nevertheless the symptoms would not be detached from the parental figures. Rather, they were "extended into" the therapy hour; consequently, no true transference neurosis could develop. During latency, especially, the analysis of the defenses may result in a reenactment of impulses related to the oedipal period but, again, in the familial context. Fifteen years later (1966), she had altered her views and recognized that a real transference neurosis could occur, but only during latency or early puberty. By this time the conflictual material has been repressed and detached from the oedipal objects and can reappear in therapy as a true transference neurosis.

Fraiberg, like Erikson, stressed the symbolic and metaphysical aspects of children's play and the importance of using the child's fantasies and metaphors as windows to repressed impulses and conflicts. Both have pointed out that the therapist's objective is to help the child achieve a level of functioning appropriate to his or her developmental age. This implies an understanding of the progression of psychosexual maturation and of the defenses available to the ego at each stage (Fraiberg, 1959).

Relationship and Play Therapies

Coincident with the evolution of the psychoanalytic treatments for young children, other approaches were evolving. In England,

Lydia Jackson and Kathleen Todd (1940) were moving away from the current psychoanalytic views of work with children. They spoke of a "therapy of play" which used play as a means of diagnosis as well as for psychological treatment. Emphasis was put on a prior investigation of the child's past history and the family setting. Less attention was given, in the treatment phase, to transference phenomena and other features of child analysis. They viewed their approach as eclectic and described it as "play therapy."

Under the influence of Rank's concept of "relationship therapy," Jessie Taft (1933) and Frederick Allen (1942) focused almost exclusively on establishing a meaningful therapeutic relationship with the child. Neither an initial diagnostic evaluation nor a consideration of family history data was deemed essential or important. Therapy was viewed as a concentrated growth experience; current emotions and feelings were explored rather than seeking their origins in past experiences. The child's resistances, aggressions, and dependencies were worked through as they occurred in the presence of the therapist without relating them back to earlier familial experiences. The important therapeutic element was deemed to be the use the child makes of the relationship with a sensitive and understanding adult. The goal was self-acceptance experienced in a growth-fulfilling relationship.

Limits were considered important by defining the boundaries of each hour and of therapy as a whole. Beginnings and endings were accorded considerable weight; the termination of therapy was seen not only as the end of an experience but as the beginning of a new phase of independence.

As an outgrowth and further extension of relationship therapy, Virginia Axline (1947) developed her method of client-centered, or nondirective, play therapy; Clark Moustakas (1953) subsequently elaborated on her theories. Stress was on total acceptance of the child in the context of a friendly, permissive relationship. Therapy was based on the premise that there is a profound pressure for growth and self-realization in all persons—children as well as adults. The child leads the way and the therapist reflects the child's feelings as verbally expressed or as reenacted in the play. Insight is achieved in this manner, rather than through analytic interpretations. There is no recognition of transference phenomena, no mention of ego functions, id, and superego, and no attempt to explore the psychodynamic sources of the child's difficulties. Diagnostic interviews, psychological assessments, and prior exploration of the child's earlier familial experiences are not considered necessary. It is felt that the child can work through his or her problems in the presence, and with the support, of an empathic, accepting adult.

Current Therapeutic Strategies

From the 1960s to date, a second generation of child therapists has evolved whose methods represent three distinct trends. At one end of the spectrum are the more recent followers of Anna Freud's methods of child analysis, with increasing emphasis on ego psychology and attention to the early developmental and libidinal stages. Representative of this approach is the continuing work of the present staff and former colleagues at the Hampton Child-Therapy Clinic (e.g., Joseph Sandler, Christoph Heinicke, Anna Maenchen, and Phyllis and Robert Tyson).

At the opposite extreme are the current practitioners of derivatives of nondirective play therapy, such as Charles Schaefer, Louise and Bernard Guerney, Richard Gardner, and John Reisman.

There now seems to be a growing movement toward a more central and eclectic position that is incorporating concepts, methods, and procedures from both poles and, perhaps, pointing to new pathways for the future. Various terms have been used for this approach: *child psychotherapy, psychodynamic psychotherapy,* and *psychoanalytically oriented child therapy.* In addition to representing a compromise between the two extremes of treatment, these midfield derivations also seem to be reflecting present-day social trends resulting from the financial constraints imposed by available sources of payment, and the time constraints of modern family life-styles. Concomitant with these trends has come increased emphasis on family and group therapies, and the need for crisis intervention (e.g., child abuse, sexual molestations, school phobias, suicide attempts) and for short-term focusing on specific problem areas (e.g., reactions to divorce, death of a parent or sibling, fire-setting, emotional components of learning disabilities).

The treatment modalities resulting from these newer trends represent a practical down-to-earth approach with attention to the probable causes of the child's unique problems, and consideration of the supportive strengths as well as the probable weaknesses in the family system. Therapy for the child is based on psychodynamic formulations derived from psychoanalytic theory but with modifications of traditional analytic procedures. Psychoanalytic concepts, such as transference, countertransference, and judicious interpretations, are recognized and incorporated into the nonanalytic therapies. There is more emphasis on the establishment of a therapeutic alliance and less on the transference relationship per se. More attention is given to ego functions and interpersonal relationships, while different therapists may emphasize, or neglect, various aspects of defenses, symbolic material, or fantasy manifestations. Due to the time constraints of shorter-term treatment, the establishment of a true transference neurosis often is neither encouraged nor facilitated.

Major recent proponents of this psychodynamically oriented, but nonanalytic, treatment include John McDermott and

Saul Harrison (1977), Shirley Cooper and Leon Wanerman (1977, 1984), and Henry Coppolillo (1987).

The author's orientation would fall within these "mixed" approaches and might best be described as ego-dynamic, based as it is on the consolidation of ego functions, and strongly influenced by psychodynamic principles. The initial emphasis in treatment is on the current state of the child's reality functioning, capacities, and defenses. As these defenses are observed and then explored, the affects being defended against become a focus of investigation. When this process is well under way, reenactments of fantasies and feeling states from earlier unresolved libidinal conflicts will appear in the child's play or behavior toward the therapist. The therapist's reflections, clarifications, and interpretations become focused on making connections between past difficulties and present unresolved conflicts. During this process the child gradually acquires the insight which accompanies growth in the capacity for self-observation, the ability to see another's point of view, and a concomitant feeling of competence appropriate for his or her age. The process of therapy, as illustrated in this presentation, uses psychoanalytic concepts in understanding the child's unconscious fantasies and symbolic productions, while meeting the child on the ego level in interpretations and reflections.

Addendum

In addition to the references for the works cited in the Introduction and elsewhere in the text, a further list of suggested readings for beginning therapists has been included at the end of this volume. This sampling of selections (largely journal articles and book chapters) focuses on the general theory, principles and procedures for psychotherapy with neurotic children of latency age.[1] Subjects covered include the classical works dealing with developmental phases and the psychosexual stages; the process of therapy (e.g., resistances, transference and countertransference, termination); symbolic interpretations of children's drawings and play representations; and various derivatives of play.

[1]Not included are selections dealing with specific referral problem areas, work with very young children, and those with borderline or psychotic characteristics.

Chapter 1

Therapeutic Principles and Preparatory Procedures

Overview of Treatment Process

Any number of theoretical approaches might have been adopted for the case to be presented here, but each therapist gradually develops a general modus operandi for his or her work. Some general aspects of treatment for anxious, neurotic children can be derived from the therapeutic process as it unfolded with this particular child.

Before treatment is begun hypotheses are formulated on the basis of information from the family history and psychological assessments. From these sources a chronology can be constructed of any traumas or difficult periods in the child's earlier experiences. These nodal points would be examined with particular attention to their occurrence and timing in connection with expected milestones in the preoedipal and oedipal phases of development. Awareness of such significant events can be used in making preliminary formulations and predictions for therapy. It is also possible to "set the stage" by providing, along with the usual assortment of play materials, those that might well elicit

11

associations and connections, such as toy animals relevant to the child's specific fears or phobias; food and baby bottles if oral deprivations were a prominent feature in the infantile history; or sand, finger paints, and gooey clay if compulsive cleanliness is an outstanding problem.

In the first phase of treatment, the focus would be on ego functions and the child's defenses and resistances as portrayed in modes of relating to the therapist and in the use of materials. As the frequently used defenses are explored, the therapist endeavors to put the child's feelings and fantasies into words, while at the same time pointing out the distancing and/or defensive maneuvers being repetitively employed. Thus the child is helped to an understanding of the habitual use of certain defenses in certain situations. As these connections are made over time, the child gradually acquires the insight that accompanies the capacity for self-observation.

In the second phase, the symbolic representations of the child's conflicts and their displacement onto play representations of self and family members become the focus of the child–therapist interaction. The unfolding pathways taken to the deeper psychosexual levels will vary with each child. Some may regress early in therapy to reenacting, through play, infantile experiences from the oral stage: extreme mother–infant symbiosis and dependency; or deprivations from an ungiving mother figure and retaliatory oral–aggressive impulses. The child may then proceed to symbolic portrayals of unresolved crises from the anal–aggressive period: overreactive concerns around dirt and cleanliness, independence–dependence conflicts, aggressive attacks, or victimization fantasies. Reworking the phallic–oedipal stage will highlight the intricacies of the affectional bond to the parent of the opposite sex as well as anxieties with respect to the rival parent, with the attendant castration fears, masturbatory anxieties, jealousies, and identification issues. Some children may work back through successive stages starting with the oedipal level; some may omit one or two levels, concentrating on the one that has proved most critical in their unique experience.

When a similar play theme has occurred repeatedly, the therapist uses this accumulation to summarize and speculate, with the child, as to the meaning and possible origins of the theme; or to point out the inconsistencies or ambivalences that are apparent. These areas are then explored, clarified, and interpreted as appropriate. While transference phenomena are recognized and acknowledged, they would not be interpreted as directly as would be the case in longer-term analytic work.

Throughout the therapeutic process the therapist remains alert to clues that would tie the material to the earlier speculations from known events in the child's past experience. While a child is not capable of free association, the therapist must engage in this process, as well as listening with the "third ear," in order to remain in tune with what the surface play may be covering up or revealing. The play may become highly symbolic, for example, reenacting fairy tales or regressing to primary process fantasy, with reversals of affect, condensations, and displacement from one object or part-object to another. At first, the therapist usually interprets within the metaphor, thus enabling the child to maintain a certain distance from the underlying disturbing impulses. Even in more "everyday" types of play enactments, the therapist may elect to keep observations and clarifications in the third-person mode, either in terms of the characters in the play or with respect to what "other children" might feel in similar situations. This once-removed approach seems to encourage children to give freer rein to their fantasy portrayals. For some children, this is as close to acknowledging reality as they can come; for the therapist to make direct connections to the child's own experiences would lead to withdrawal from the play theme and a retreat from self-revelation. Other children will feel comfortable in shifting to the first-person framework as the therapist moves to suggesting that the child may also have had experiences or feelings similar to those of the play characters.

As the child works through the earlier conflicts and their accompanying unconscious impulses, the ego gradually takes its rightful place as moderator between id and superego. There is a noticeable enhancement of ego capacities with reasoned assessments of object relations, realistic evaluations of self, and the achievement of self-acceptance and a feeling of competence.

In summary, the route taken has been from a focus on ego functions and defensive resistances, to exploration of the underlying primary process affective ties from earlier developmental levels, and back again to a consolidation of the personality at the level of secondary process.

How does one assess change, or readiness for termination? Frequently there is a spontaneous expression from the child that he or she no longer feels the need to continue; other after-school activities are more compelling; or spontaneous comparisons will be made between the old self and the new self. There is a diminution of the referral symptoms and an improvement in social adjustment and peer relations. The therapist is treated as a separate "real" person, and interchanges between therapist and child are more on a peer to peer basis. Fantasy and symbolic play are reduced and replaced by age-adequate interests and preoccupations.

At the same time, it is also hoped that the therapist is prepared to let go, with the objective recognition of the child's gains and the expectation that the child can continue to build on a more conflict-free foundation.

Referral Problems and Family History

Don, eight years, eight months at the time of evaluation, was the second of three boys; the first child (Joe) was just one year older than Don, while the youngest was two years of age. Although of above-average intelligence, Don would soon be repeating second grade. During his kindergarten year it was necessary to change schools in midterm; both boys had wanted to continue in their old school. Also it was at about this time that the little brother was born. Don did very well in first grade and was at the head of his class. During the following year he seemed to lose his self-confidence, daydreamed a lot, became very nervous, was biting his nails, and ended up at the bottom of his class. Although earlier he had liked sports, he had recently been avoiding participation.

Don's infantile history was quite traumatic. He was delivered, placenta previa, at eight months, weighing only four and a half pounds. He was fed intravenously for the first five weeks, and brought home from the hospital at seven weeks. There was a urethral stricture at birth, which necessitated an operation at six months of age with the insertion of a urethral probe for three months; this resulted in episodes of "blood streaming out." Currently, he is subject to nosebleeds. Four months before clinic referral, Don and his little brother each had an elective tonsillectomy and adenoidectomy (T&A) because the oldest brother needed to have his tonsils out. (At that time, such elective surgery was not generally accepted medical practice.)

Since Don's birth, mother had had several miscarriages in addition to the successful pregnancy two years before referral. When Don was four, she had an abortion, with much hemorrhaging, and Don remembered that. Within the year before referral (during which time Don's school difficulties commenced), mother had a tubal pregnancy and was hospitalized for one week; father spent a week in the hospital with ulcers; an aunt had a ruptured appendix, then a second operation two weeks later; one month after this episode the three boys had their T&As as mentioned above.

Don would become frightened when ill, nauseated when

given shots, and hysterical with his frequent nosebleeds. He was very susceptible to falls, which often resulted in a cut lip. As a result, his lips had become somewhat thickened, and his older brother would tease him about this. He was wetting the bed about once a month. He was very meticulous about his clothes, refusing to wear anything patched or soiled; if a shirt became dirty he would either change it immediately or put clean ones on top (up to as many as five at one time). Don was sharing a room with his older brother who teased and ridiculed him repeatedly.

Mother, thirty-one, admitted to being disappointed when she learned she was pregnant with Don since the older boy would be only one year old. She definitely hoped this second child would be a girl, and may have tended to feminize him. She did report that she cried when he started kindergarten. Father, thirty-two, owned and operated several service stations and enjoyed drag racing; mother was fearful for his safety. Father felt Don was a "hindrance to the family." He would punish him with a strap occasionally. When Don was restricted or deprived as a punishment, he would tell his parents that he "didn't want it anyway." In general the family appeared to be functioning satisfactorily, although divorce was considered at one point early in the marriage.

Summary of Referral Symptoms

In addition to the persistent fear of blood, Don is generally fearful and passive, shows low self-esteem, and retreats to daydreaming. His schoolwork deteriorated markedly in the year before referral. He now avoids sports and camaraderie with his peers. He is compulsively neat, bites his nails, and occasionally wets his bed.

Psychological Evaluation

Projective testing, utilizing the Rorschach, the House-Tree-Person (H-T-P) drawing test, and the Thematic Apperception Test (TAT), was administered before the child was recommended for psychotherapy. Unfortunately, it was not possible to obtain the psychologist's specific scoring for the Rorschach; the recorded inquiry material was not extensive enough to permit adequate scoring of the protocol subsequently. Nevertheless, main trends and overriding character traits can be highlighted from the responses.

In presenting the Rorschach protocol, pertinent words and phrases with possible relevance to the case history material have been italicized for emphasis. For the H-T-P and the TAT, the possible relationship of the child's comments to the actuality of his problems and home life are indicated in the marginal comments.

The summaries following each test protocol are post hoc evaluations and impressions of the author, and were made subsequent to the termination of therapy. While it is highly possible that her views were influenced by knowledge of the events of therapy, nevertheless every relationship highlighted reflects material from the case history. The fact that play sequences from therapy reemphasize revelations from the test material only reiterates the usefulness of rereading test protocols at intervals while the therapy is ongoing. If material from the play sessions reinforces test responses, both sources gain added validity as reflections of the child's underlying dynamics. Conversely, if there were no correspondence between test responses and subsequent therapeutic events one might wonder whether the therapy was really reaching the core of the child's problems. Test responses can serve as an initial guide, or searchlight, to point to aspects to be explored in therapy, particularly those responses that appear to highlight known aspects from the case history. In effect, one moves from case history, to projective testing, to incidents in therapy, in the quest for an understanding of the child's problems and for progress toward their solution.

TABLE 1.1
Rorschach

		Free Association		Inquiry
I.	1.	A goat.	1.	*Horns, nose,* ears, *eyes.*
	2.	Could be a wolf, too.	2.	It's best as a wolf.
	3.	Space ship (card inverted).	3.	Legs that it lands on, *holes where fuel comes out* (Ss).
II.	1.	A hippie.	1.	*Eyes, mouth* (S), beard (lower red).
	2.	Sun (card inverted).	2.	Round shape (same area as beard).
	3.	Ear.	3.	But too long (upper red).
III.	1.	People lifting bowling balls.	1.	*Women* because of shoes.
	2.	Two *big eyes.*		
	3.	Monster (card inverted).	3.	*Nose, teeth,* just the head.
	4.	Two *stupid guys* kicking a football (card inverted).	4.	(Why stupid?) Because of faces, one leg's up, kicking, and one leg is down.
	5.	Monkey *face.*	5.	(Upper side red.)
IV.	1.	*Giant* with big feet.	1.	(Excludes bottom D.)

2. Caterpillar.

3. Decoration or crown (card inverted).

V. 1. Butterfly with antennae.
2. Could be a hawk, with *mouth* open (card sideways).
3. Bat.

4. Could be a duck (card opposite sideways).
5. Crocodile.

VI. 1. Animal skin with whiskers and face part.
2. Fur.

3. Could be a *drill*; a thing to drill and handles (card inverted).

VII. 1. (After long scrutiny) Looks like two elephant heads but ears are not big enough (card inverted).
2. Could be a decoration (card inverted).

3. Tiger *nose*, neck.

2. Things *sticking out* of its body (bottom D).
3. (Top of center D.)

3. Really isn't a bird, it's a mouse.

5. (Tip of side projection.)

2. The color of it (rubbed card).
3. (Side projections are handles.)

1. (Center third of blot.)

2. Like on the other side; like going to the zoo. (An archway?)
3. (Upper third of blot.)

	4.	A rabbit (card inverted).	4.	(Lower third, poorly perceived.)	

VIII. 1. Could be a person, thinking, *plugging their ears* (card inverted).

     1. Hair; maybe had a headache (center orange-pink section).

    2. Something like a wolf or raccoon.

     2. (Usual side pink.)

IX. 1. A decoration.

   2. Could be *eyes* if you turn it.

    2. *Funny eyes*, not from animals or people (four center slits).

   3. Deer *horns*.

    3. (Top center orange extensions.)

   4. Four-headed *ogre* (card inverted).

    4. Whole (four pink sections are heads).

X. 1. Spiders.

    1. The legs (blue side details).

   2. Sea horse, maybe.

    2. Way around and that (side pink detail).

   3. Could be a *baby* deer.

    3. *Eyes* and little *horns* and face so pink and light skin (pale green center area of lower green detail).

   4. *Snakes,* kind of swerved.

    4. *Eyes* really are part of the deer, but are for the snake too (sides of lower green detail).

   5. Sea horses, when upside down (card inverted).

    5. Couldn't be regular horses (entire lower green detail).

Rorschach Analysis

The overall picture from the Rorschach is of a boy who is extremely constricted (high F + %, low M, and no FC or CF), cautious and careful in his approach (thirty-seven responses with high emphasis on details). He reacts in a compulsive, conscientious fashion, exploring all possibilities amid much card turning, and emphasizing common popular responses (seven out of thirty-seven) in the interest of conformity to what he perceives as expected behavior. Fantasy and creativity are held in tight control (low M, no CF or Fc, one F $\longleftrightarrow$ C) since emotional situations arouse too much anxiety. There is some evidence of insecurity and feelings of inadequacy (S responses on the first two cards).[1]

There are no FM responses, again suggesting lack of free access to creativity and "childishness." The presence of three M responses in the absence of any FM points to a pseudomaturity that is masking anxiety, inferiority feelings, and poor self-concept. Of these three M responses, the context of the first suggests some feminine identification ("women's shoes," Card III), the next is derogatory in tone ("two stupid guys," also on Card III), and the third indicates blocking out, or isolating oneself from, the world ("plugging their ears," Card VIII).

Reactions to the emotional aspects of the colored cards are noteworthy for their avoidance and denial. In view of the boy's known history of nosebleeds, bloody urethral probes in infancy, his fear of blood, and his knowledge of his mother's hemorrhaging during her frequent miscarriages, it is significant that he exhibits color shock on the two "red" cards (II and III), with no mention of the color involved when he does use the red area for

---

[1]See Halpern (1953) for further explanation of Rorschach scoring dimensions and the interpretation of Rorschach records from young children.

a hippie's "beard" and the "sun" (sunset?) on Card II, both of which could be influenced by the redness. On Card III, color is overlooked entirely with the concept of a "monkey face."

His responses to the last three colored cards are also marked by the avoidance of color. His first response to Card VIII is "a person thinking, plugging their ears." (Is he thus denying the visual impact of the color?) Unfortunately, no inquiry responses are listed for the first reaction to Card IX, "a decoration"; the use of color might well have been a factor at this point. On the final Card X, his efforts at blocking out the emotional impact of the color disintegrate under the phallic connotations of the area upon which he concentrates for the last three responses. Here he perseverates in the lower green area and melds together the concepts of a baby deer, snakes, and sea horses, with the first two sharing the same eyes (almost a contamination) along with the forced use of color and the almost textural reaction to the baby deer's "face so pink and light skin" (a color projection of pink in a pale green area).[2] The last response of "sea horses" (card upside down) shares the same total area as the baby deer and the snakes. Taken together, these final responses suggest extreme sensitivity and overwhelming anxiety, which he feels unable to handle.

Turning to content, the human figures involving movement have been discussed above. Nonactive humans either have a derogatory flavor ("hippie," Card II), or are of frightening pseudohuman characters ("monster," Card III; "giant," Card IV; "four-headed ogre," Card IX). Card VII, generally viewed as the "mother card," elicits no human responses but two rather unattractive (unfeminine?) animals, only the heads of "ele-

---

[2]Klopfer, Ainsworth, Klopfer, and Holt (1954) state, when discussing the projection, by adults, of color on a blot area of a different color: "the fantasy-dominated quality of the response suggests a serious loosening of the ties with reality and an inappropriate manifestation of affect" (p. 339).

phants" and a "tiger," followed by a poorly perceived "rabbit." He concludes this card with the curiously impersonal, nonhuman "decoration," which he elaborates as something seen when going to the zoo (probably an entrance arch). Is mother seen as a cold and awesome "opening" through which beastly animals (infants) can emerge? While there was at least one card inversion for each of the other blots, it is perhaps noteworthy that this reaction occurred for three of the four responses to the "mother card" (VII). Apparently this card also had the longest initial reaction time, and the final response ("a rabbit") was the only instance where the examiner made a note that the response was poorly perceived.

Quite prominent are the six "eye" responses starting with eyes as part of the usual facial characteristics (Cards I and II), then a pair of isolated "big eyes" (Card III), followed again by isolated "funny eyes" which are neither animal nor human (Card IX), to the final merging of a baby deer's eyes with those of a snake in the same area of Card X. Such a preponderance of "eye" percepts suggests suspiciousness and feelings of being watched, with the attendant guilt feelings. (In an adult record these responses would point to possible paranoid tendencies.)

Noses are mentioned in three cards (but only in the context of facial features) in the percepts of heads of a goat, a monster, and a tiger, giving no clues to his known concerns in this area (nosebleeds). Mouths were seen but with no specific details of lips. (He is reported to be sensitive to his brother's teasing him about his big lips.) Both mouth responses utilize the white areas to indicate open mouths (on the "hippie," Card II, and the "hawk," Card V). The three "horn" responses may be significant as indications of preoccupation with displaced phallic symbols. The first appears on the initial response to Card I ("a goat with horns, nose, ears, and eyes") where the inclusion of two items from his possible conflict areas are combined in a card generally regarded as revealing concepts of self. "Deer horns" are seen in

Card IX and again on Card X as part of his most anxiety-laden reaction (as previously described in the discussion of his color responses).

Finally, the "drill" response ("a thing to drill with handles," Card VI) elicits imagery of the painful and bloody urethral probes to which he was subjected in infancy. Considering that this follows a cF response of "fur" and his rubbing of the card, one also wonders about castration and masturbatory concerns. It is worth noting that the only other cF response occurs on Card X when he reacts in this same sensitive fashion ("pink face and light skin" of a baby deer) in his most disorganized response of the entire protocol. This is followed by the classically phallic snake whose eyes meld with those of the baby deer, suggesting the source of his strong guilt feelings. (In view of the material that subsequently emerged during therapy, such as the "blind butler" episode with its strong overtones of castration fears and oedipal conflict, and the suggestions of masturbatory impulses in the Slinky and water-balloon play, the responses to the blots take on added significance.)

TABLE 1.2

House-Tree-Person

Inquiry	Interpretive Comments
House: *(Description: Shingles on roof with shading; window panes, curtains, objects in windows; door; fence)*	
Old man and lady live in it; they have a black cat. It's an old house, not very nice.	*Home is not a pleasant place.*
A tornado blew it down, but the man and lady were in their car. The cat said the house blew away.	*There are forces beyond one's control.*

Tree: *(Description: "A weeping willow"; heavy shading; large trunk; short branches)*

A squirrel lived in it but he didn't like it because it "weeped." The squirrel had 1000 nuts. The lady screamed because the squirrel was eating the nuts.

Life is sad.

Mother figure is orally depriving.

The squirrel ran away; said he didn't live anywhere. The judge said he knew where he lived and put him in jail. He was supposed to live in his own house even if he didn't like it.

Wants to leave home and get away from unpleasant situation. Father knows best.

One has to conform and accept one's fate.

Boy: *(Description: Drew details of clothing, including pant fly and pocket, before facial features)*

Everybody talks about his big shoes. He asked his mother why she bought him such big shoes. She said because he had such big feet. Kids tease him and call him "Big Feet."

Mother is insensitive.

Or "Big Lips"? (Brother teases him about his lips.)

He dreamed he had real little feet. When he was fourteen he didn't feel so bad; he wasn't teased then because his feet were OK for a fourteen-year-old.

Hopes to grow out of his difficulties; seeks logical, realistic solutions.

Girl: *(Description: Drew face and features first; pocket closed with button; top of dress shaded)*

She lost her doll; she'd had it for days and liked it. Her brother threw it in the trash and burned it.

Things never turn out right, and brother teases.

People take advantage of a weakling.

Her mother tried to fix it but the girl didn't think it looked like her, so mother bought a new one.

Sexual anxieties and concern about mother's miscarriages?

Overall Impressions From the Drawings

Predominant is a pessimistic outlook on life: home is not a pleasant place, bad things are continually happening, brothers and peers tease. Consequently Don feels inadequate and victimized. There is considerable anxiety as indicated by heavy shading on three of the drawings. Some of his concerns center around mother's miscarriages (dolls destroyed and replaced). Mother is nurturant with babies but is seen as insensitive and orally depriving with her sons. Compulsive tendencies are evidenced in his preoccupation with details and numbers. Generally, the story endings reflect efforts at restitution, acceptance of one's fate, and hopes that things will get better in the future, all of which would be suggestive of a positive prognosis.

TABLE 1.3
TAT

Stories	Interpretive Comments
Card 1. *(A young man is contemplating a violin which rests on a table in front of him.)*[3]	
His little brother broke his violin. The child wanted one for Christmas but he didn't get it.	*Brother teases; toys are broken; he always gets the short end of things.*
Card 4. *(A woman is clutching the shoulders of a man whose face and body are averted as if he were trying to pull away from her.)*	
The man is going to the army. They've had a baby.	*Preoccupation with births.*

[3]Card descriptions are taken from Bellak, L. (1971), *The T.A.T. and C.A.T. in Clinical Use*, 2nd ed. New York: Grune & Stratton, pp. 48, 51, 52, 56, 57.

Card 5. *(A middle-aged woman is standing on the threshold of a half-opened door looking into a room.)*

The lady is thinking about her dog, "Waggie." She got it at the dog pound.	*Mother likes dogs (children?).*

Card 7BM. *(A gray-haired man is looking at a younger man who is sullenly staring into space.)*

The man was in a car wreck. His boy ran to him and took him to the hospital. They towed the car to a body shop. They operated on the man; he had a broken arm and a cut on his head.	*Father drag-races—concern for his safety. Bloody head (nose, lips?)*

Card 17BM. *(A naked man is clinging to a rope. He is in the act of climbing up or down.)*

It's a circus. One man fell; he landed on the trampoline. The other man is going to see if he's OK. Then they both go back up.	*Again, concern about injuries to others, or to self?*

Card 13B. *(A little boy is sitting on the doorstep of a log cabin.)*

He's thinking about a new horse. His father gave him a pony. He was on a sleigh one night in the forest and couldn't find his way back. His mother and father had breakfast, but he didn't have any.	*Wants more than he gets. Feels he was at fault and so deserved the oral deprivation.*
	Father is concerned, protective, nurturant.
His father walked three days trying to find him, but the boy got further and further into the woods.	*Happy ending.*
Father finally found him. Father and the boy went home for breakfast. He spent the whole night thinking he wanted a bicycle.	*Accepts fate; settles for a bike as less dangerous than horse or pony.*

Card 16. *(Blank card)*

The mouse hated cheese and chased cats and scared dogs. His mousehole had five bedrooms. He lived alone and chased the others out. Everyone called him the "screwed-up, mixed-up mouse."

Oppositional and counterphobic; a loner.

Negative self-concept; is teased and picked on by peers.

His cousin wanted to live with him because he was like him only meaner. They went to the jungle and saw a kangaroo. They thought it was a gigantic mouse. The kangaroo threw them to the gorilla, the gorilla to the zebra, the zebra to the ostrich, the ostrich to the giraffe, but the giraffe missed.

Children are helpless in the hands of adults.

The mouse ran away but saw a snake egg and gave it to the giraffe. The egg broke and out came hundreds of snakes and he chased all of them.

Pregnancy fantasy (mother's many pregnancies).

He used the ostrich egg for a boat. He sailed and walked to the palace to tell his cousin. The cousin didn't believe him and kicked him out. The other cousin went to Africa. They kicked the cousin out and brought all the people back.

Oceanic feelings and fantasies before being kicked out into the real world. All ends happily.

Overall Impressions From the TAT

Concerns about birth and birth fantasies are again in evidence. Relationships to the mother figures are somewhat distant in comparison to father's protectiveness and the child's concerns over his safety. One could speculate that this concern may be masking a death wish. On the other hand, it may be just too dangerous to identify with father if that would mean having to participate in his risky (aggressive) activities. (Further light is thrown on the sources of his unresolved oedipal and identification problems by the case-history information that mother had hoped he would be a girl.)

Added to his difficulties is the feeling that he is constantly being picked on and teased by his older brother and peers, and that things never turn out the way he would like. He finally resolves the dilemma, not by adopting an obvious feminine stance, but by passive withdrawal and becoming a loner. But this solution only brings on more teasing.

His difficulties in achieving an adequate masculine concept of self, and the inhibition of his aggressive drives, must be strong contributors to his learning difficulties in spite of his above-average intellectual capacities.

As with the drawings, the stories generally end on a positive note with acceptance of the realities of each situation, thus demonstrating considerable ego strength and the ability to tackle and surmount his present difficulties.

Composite Summary of the Projective Testing

The TAT and H-T-P lend added emphasis to Don's low self-esteem and withdrawal from peers. Identification figures are seen as helpless, ineffective, and insecure. He feels he deserves the bad luck and punishments that come his way. Home is not a pleasant place, with mother, especially, and father meting out oral deprivations. Brother and peers tease and isolate him. Mother is generally viewed as being insensitive while father is portrayed as more concerned and protective. In turn, the boy figures express concern for father's injuries and accidents, yet evidences of identification with father are notable for their absence. Pregnancies and successive multiple births are alluded to in both protocols. In spite of all of the above, situations are usually resolved to everyone's satisfaction; no one is ever permanently damaged; story endings are positive and realistic. The capacity for mastery and autonomous ego functioning is clearly indicated.

As would be expected, the Rorschach reveals the deeper underlying personality dynamics and the defenses employed. His constricted and cautiously conforming view of the world is a prominent feature of the protocol. He engages in compulsive maneuvers that limit expressions of creativity and highlight his insecurity and feelings of inferiority. His identification is ambivalent at best; his views of women are not very flattering and men are seen as "stupid guys." He attempts to control emotionally loaded situations by denial or avoidance, but eventually his high degree of anxiety breaks through in disorganzied and illogical responses. His phallic–urethral concerns (and past history) are revealed via displacement to horns, drills, and snakes. The frequent references to "eyes" indicate feelings of guilt, which may possibly be associated with masturbatory activity as suggested by the juxtaposition of several relevant percepts in the responses to the final blot.

Turning to a consideration of the defenses at his disposal, *Repression* is marked with a high number of form responses on the Rorschach, few movement percepts, and no well-structured color responses, all implying a strong but brittle ego that must exert great effort to maintain conscious control of his affective life. These rigid controls break down in the final Card X with the forced use of color combined with sensitivity to the "feel" of the percept.

Denial is clearly displayed in the avoidance of color on the colored Rorschach cards, as well as the misnaming of the one color description given. Noses and mouths, the two known areas of concern, are almost casually mentioned in the context of facial descriptions, while reactions and responses to the "mother card" suggest that considerable anxiety was aroused and suppressed.

Projection, one of the most primitive defenses, is revealed in the numerous "eye" responses, suggesting feelings of being under surveillance and, as mentioned above, unwittingly leading to a revelation of the possible sources of guilt.

There is considerable *Undoing*, with numerous reinterpretations of percepts, giving and denying responses, such as "it could be this . . . or that" on the Rorschach. In addition, several incidents occur in the TAT where alternate solutions are proposed. *Compulsive* maneuvers feature prominently as a means of blocking out unpleasant thoughts or uncomfortable feelings. Noteworthy is his obsessive preoccupation with the commonly straightforward Card V to which he gives five responses while turning the card in various positions. Obsessive use of counting and numbers also appears in the H-T-P and the TAT.

Evidences of one of the more mature defenses, *Intellectualization*, are minimal on the Rorschach but do appear with the H-T-P and TAT. Here they throw light on his inherent ego intactness and his ability to make the best of bad situations.This capacity should enable him eventually to achieve a higher level of independent functioning.

Possible Determinants of Symptoms

Effects of Bodily Insults

From the moment of birth Don has been the subject of, or has been caught up in, one medical trauma after another. His premature birth and low birth weight necessitated hospitalization for his first two months of life, with intravenous feeding for the initial five weeks. He was thus deprived of any early affectional closeness with his mother and any comfort from breast or bottle. At the age of six months he was returned to the hospital for the urinary operation that necessitated further intrusive procedures (urethral probe and its attendant bleeding) over the next three months. Bleeding has persisted in the form of frequent nosebleeds and cuts to his lips (displacement upward from genital to facial openings). The most recent attack on his body integrity occurred during the year before referral—an elective T&A under circumstances that could only add to his feelings of helplessness.

The regressive pull of illness and hospitalizations has resulted in continued dependency on his mother; his early oral conflicts and deprivations were undoubtedly reactivated by the T&A. The reality of the T&A, in turn, reinforces the more deeply buried sense of damage and bodily injury resulting from the urethral traumas in infancy. Does he also view the original operation as a demonstration that his parents were dissatisfied with him from the very start? Were they in fact, with symbolic castration, trying to change him into the girl that they had wished for? In any event, with this latest oral insult he has now been proven to be vulnerable to attacks from below and above. To hide further exposure of his weaknesses he must retreat from active interaction with his peers, act stupid at school, and withdraw from the usual boyhood pursuits which would have given him a feeling of competence and masculinity. No one must "see" his true self.

Illnesses of Other Family Members

His mother has had frequent miscarriages, including an abortion, when he was four, at which time he is reported to have been very much aware of her hemorrhaging. Such experiences undoubtedly generate feelings of guilt (was I responsible?) and/or fears of her possible destructiveness to all of her children. Also, one can easily imagine the effect on this young boy as he listens to the probable discussions and comments from friends and relatives, which would be made more acute if mother's continued wish to have a daughter were also emphasized. (Cain, Erickson, Fast, and Vaughan [1964] point out that children whose mothers have miscarried may blame the mother for destroying the baby and so fear her potential for violence; they may blame themselves for having played too roughly with her, made too much noise, or not helped her enough. They may feel that they have not been "good enough" so that mother wanted a replacement, or that they were the wrong sex and so she was trying again.)

The year before referral must have been particularly traumatic, with mother's terminated tubal pregnancy, father's hospitalization for ulcers, and an aunt's two operations for a ruptured appendix. In the midst of these demonstrations of physical vulnerability, Don and his two brothers have their worst fears turned into reality as they also find themselves in the hospital for the T&As. The family's tremendous preoccupation with bodily illnesses and operations in this one year undoubtedly contributed to, or precipitated, the sharp decline in Don's school performance during the year before referral. It is also little wonder that he now responds to any bodily invasion (shots, cuts, nosebleeds) with hysterical fear.

Relations to Parents and Siblings

Rather than displaying overt feminine behavior, Don seems to have responded to mother's expressed wish that he had been a girl by passivity, cleanliness, virtuousness, and conformity to her wishes. He is caught between the urge to be passive, and so please mother, and the struggle to break away and assert his masculinity, with the former in the ascendence and the latter smoldering underneath. Again, does he see the mother's frequent (but unsuccessful) attempts to have more children as further demonstrating her profound wish to have a girl? Ipso facto both he and his younger brother have disappointed her. Comments of friends and relatives to this effect would only confirm his sex as being a disappointment to her.

His robust, drag-racing father occasionally resorts to physical punishment and is strict and rejecting, presenting a formidable obstacle to identification. Father undoubtedly favors the elder son, thus further pairing Don off with his mother.

The older brother teases Don unmercifully and, like the father, constantly downgrades him. To aggravate the situation further, the two boys share a bedroom. It seems quite probable that Don would be subjected to considerable verbal abuse on those occasions when he wets his bed. Feelings of shame originate from the attitudes of family members toward incontinence—urethral or anal. To have his brother be a constant witness to his lapses would be unusually painful.

Little mention is made of the much younger brother, but the fact that he was another boy would have reactivated a sense of mother's rejection of the male sex. This child was born during Don's kindergarten year, when separation problems had already become acute (at least on the mother's part when Don started school), and when a change of schools (and a change of homes?) was necessitated in midterm. It is remarkable that Don did so well in school the next year (head of his class in first grade). It was not until the following year, and after the additional medical traumas, that major difficulties apparently surfaced.

Predictions for Therapy

Before initiating therapy, and after careful review of the case history material and test results, it is helpful to conduct a preview of possible directions in which the therapy might move. In Don's case one could predict considerable preoccupation with, and fear of, blood, operations, and things medical. Yet considering that such references were largely absent (denied?) in the projective tests, the therapist would need to be alert to any openings whereby this subject could be introduced.

In view of the early urinary operation and probes, it seems likely that his concerns about blood may well be related to far deeper, less conscious fantasies associated with the genital area, such as castration anxieties or masturbatory activities. His probable need to reassure himself that his body parts are still intact may account for the emphasis, in the Rorschach, on body protrusions, horns, noses, and "things sticking out," and may be the source of the suspiciousness and guilt feelings also suggested by the Rorschach.

The bed-wetting was not presented as a particularly major problem, yet it is present. His compulsive neatness suggests that the early toilet-training period may have been traumatic, in that he now appears to be covering up, with reaction formation, his infantile urges to assert control and/or to compete with father on a urethral level. However, there is little evidence from the projective material that would indicate extremely obsessive preoccupations, or that his compulsiveness has become a well-developed, repetitive, and immobilizing response to most real-life situations. The introduction of "messy" activities is called for with the goal of loosening him up and freeing him from his tight internal constraints.

The massive oral deprivations of infancy undoubtedly distorted his attachment to mother when he was a baby, and may have delayed or adversely affected progress through the oedipal period. Mother figures (dolls and puppets) may be seen as bad, withholding, and feared objects, rather than as loving and someone to be loved. Direct or symbolic references to pregnancies and births should be looked for and pursued. Jealousy of the younger brother may also play a larger role than is evident from the workup.

There are few indications of any identification with father, yet a truly feminine orientation is not apparent either. Father figures on the TAT are viewed as in danger of being destroyed as a result of their masculine activities; in essence, it would just be too dangerous to emulate father. This whole area, as well as the effect his seemingly overwhelming older brother is having on the development of a viable masculine identification, should be explored.

Chapter 2

The Therapy Hours

Introduction

Psychiatric and psychological evaluations and the social history workup were completed in mid-August. Psychotherapy was begun in mid-September when Don was eight years, nine months of age. There were thirty-one weekly sessions throughout the school year, until the end of May, with one more follow-up session at the end of the summer.

The child's therapist was a female clinical psychologist. The mother was also seen weekly by a male child psychiatrist, with father joining them occasionally.

Playroom Equipment

Although the playroom contained the usual assortment of toys and supplies, certain items appeared to be especially pertinent for this case and, when necessary, were placed in strategic positions as therapy progressed. A doctor's kit was deemed to be essential, as were paints (primary colors, green, and black). The playroom

37

was equipped with a standing easel large enough for holding large sheets of newsprint (18″ x 24″), large jars of poster paint, and long-handled brushes with half-inch bristles.[1] Clay, finger paints, water, a dishpan full of sand, and water pistols would stimulate anal–urethral play, while the small "Slinky" spiral toys could be used as phallic symbols.

Parental figures would be provided through the dollhouse dolls and the puppets (especially a witch for a bad-mother figure, a queen or princess for a good mother, and a king or policeman for a father surrogate).[2]

Finally, in view of the early oral deprivations, a baby bottle should be available, and an endless supply of cookies. Vanilla wafers or butter cookies are recommended rather than candies and chocolates. Some children are allergic to chocolate, parents may object to too many sweets, and the child can consume more "items" of cookies before feeling physically satiated. (For further discussion of the inclusion of food in therapy, see Haworth and Keller [1962, 1964].)

Fortunately, a small bathroom containing a toilet and lavatory opened directly off one end of the playroom.

Explanation of Process Notes

The basic text presents a running account of the actions and activities during each hour and the child's (C) comments accompanying his play. The indented paragraphs indicate the therapist's (T) comments, observations, and interpretations as made to the child. In those instances where the therapist's comments and the

[1]Small sheets of paper and the usual tins of water colors with small brushes do not lend themselves to active, vigorous expression of strong emotional themes.

[2]The rubberized sets of family puppet figures seem to be much too realistic, and threatening, to most children. Consequently these are not viewed as suitable media for eliciting optimal levels of projection for intrafamilial conflicts.

child's responses were intricately intertwined, the entire inter-change is included in the indented section. Obviously the therapist offered verbal commentaries far more frequently than is indicated here; only those that, at the close of the hour, seemed to have helped or hindered the progress of therapy were recorded as an integral part of the process notes for that hour.

The right column consists of the marginal notes added by the therapist after each session's report was typed. These brief words or phrases represent her speculations and free associations as to the possible meaning of the various play sequences, and her thoughts as to the symbolic aspects of the play characters and activities. Following such a procedure enables the therapist to quickly scan the previous sessions, and thus to place the current session in context and continuity with those that preceded it.

The initial session of therapy has been discussed frequently in the literature as providing, in capsulated form, an overview of the child's problems and some indication of the direction in which the therapy may move. In Don's case, it took two sessions to demonstrate this phenomenon. In order to highlight the various pertinent aspects of these two sessions, addenda by the author have been included after the process notes for each of the first two sessions.

An interim progress report was prepared after the first eighteen sessions and a final overall summary report after the termination of therapy. These are inserted at the appropriate places. Comments and observations of the child psychiatrist who treated the mother are also included at the end of this section.

Process Notes, Sessions 1–18

Session 1

Don came to the clinic directly from school and was immaculately dressed in a pressed shirt, necktie, jacket, and clean pants. (He attends public school, so no "uniform" as such is required.) He is a good-looking, healthy-appearing lad who seems shy and somewhat ill at ease. He is quiet and passive, but not effeminate in attitudes or gestures.

T structured the sessions as to time and place; only she would be seeing him; this would be different from the testing sessions where he was asked many questions; here he could do whatever he wanted. When asked if he knew why he was coming, Don said because of his nervousness and being slow. On being questioned later, he said he was slow in school and in getting things done. T said they would work together on these things, that it seems to help children to have someone they can be with and talk to each week.

Don spent the entire time with the dart guns. At first he showed no affect when the darts missed the target and not much elation when he was successful, until T commented on this. Then he became somewhat more animated. He remained very methodical in his approach throughout, shooting all of the darts before

Constrained and compulsive

retrieving those that fell, taking careful aim, etc. Finally he checked out each gun and each dart, setting aside those that didn't work properly.

He volunteered that he and his cousin had spent a whole day making a target and shooting darts. His mother doesn't allow them to shoot indoors; in fact she doesn't allow him to own a dart gun.

States parental restrictions. Is therapy too permissive?

He noticed the water pistol on the shelf and exclaimed in surprise that we had them. "I bet the kids really get soaked with those." T asked whether he had one or had ever used one. He said his friends didn't have them but he had seen lots of them in the stores. Kids didn't seem to be buying them because the store was always changing the price; first they would be 20¢, then 30¢, then 20¢, so you never knew how much money you would need to have with you.

Would like to be able to "let go" but denies his feelings and rationalizes— all in the third person.

Toward the end of the hour T again structured the sessions; he would be coming every week, everything would be just between him and T; "I guess this seems different from anything you've ever done before." He smiled assent.

He walked off down the hall far ahead of T and sat down in the waiting room to wait for his mother.

Author's observations on first session. It frequently happens in therapy with young children that the first session's choices of toys and activities restate, in the child's terms, the problems and concerns that have brought him (or her) into therapy. Don selected the darts (a potentially intrusive toy), but now he is in control. His use of the dart gun mirrors his reported day-to-day behavior—compulsive, methodical, and totally lacking in spontaneity. On the other hand, this may be a function of the newness of the situation in the presence of a strange adult. He also lets her know that mother has other standards that he must abide by, while at the same time expressing uneasiness at the liberal situation in which he now finds himself.

His comments about the water pistol again expose his uneasiness and serve to mask his probable unconscious delight in the gun's possibilities. These, of course, would tie into, and trigger, urination fantasies and his control problems. He handles the dilemma by a series of denials and rationalizations, which then lead to a preoccupation with numbers and prices in an obsessive effort to maintain control.

Session 2

Puppets were in the room today, and cookies. T explained that the cookies were there for him, and he could have as many as he wished. He made no response and did not eat any, but some interesting reactions occurred later in the session (see below).

Don spent the entire time with the puppets enacting numerous sequences. He always put the puppets he had used back in the box, then took out those to be used next (often some he had just used). The witch, alligator, and devil were used most, with the witch appearing in almost all the scenes. She would change the other animals into meaner or gentler species and was generally the one in control.

Neat and compulsive

Witch = mother

In one scene a man lured each animal into joining his parade, only to cage them all and cart them off to the zoo.

The king married the queen, then looked for a pet to give her; in the process each gentle animal was changed into a wild one.

Pet = child

Three witches all went looking for a husband. When a man was found—the devil, a pirate—at least two of the witches would fight over him with one always being eliminated.

Probably the most meaningful scenes were those that incorporated the dollhouse. But first he was careful to remove all the dollhouse dolls and put them on a shelf so "the other kids could find them if they wanted to use them." In the

Rationalizes his compulsiveness

dollhouse sequences he was definitely identifying with the alligator puppet. It has a very long,
hard snout which opens to reveal a bright red
lining—very phallic and "damaged" looking.
First the alligator married the dog, then the dog
went on a trip and the alligator got the monkey to
act as maid and cook his dinner. The monkey
made a brew with garlic and pepper in it, and
poured this down the alligator's mouth, burning
and stinging it.

*Alligator =
self*

*Sensations
related to
urethral probes*

T reflected how the "good" food actually turns
out to be bad, how his mouth must hurt, it
really stings.

Then the monkey changed all the furniture
around. The dog–wife came back and was not
too upset with the change, but there was not
room enough for both "women" so the monkey
had to leave.

Don smiled while T talked about how a man
could only have one woman around at a time.

In another sequence the witch wanted a "gigantic " bathroom, so she moved all the bathroom furniture into the largest room and crowded
all the kitchen furniture into the smallest room.

T commented on the relative values involved,
with a small kitchen she couldn't cook as good
meals, and the bathroom seems more important to her.

Then the witch messed the furniture up more. A guest came who really put things in a turmoil, piling the refrigerator and sink onto a bed, plugging up the doorway with the tub, and making everything helter skelter. Immediately Don started to put all the furniture back in the logical rooms.

Spontaneity triggers guilt and anxiety

T reflected it seemed like it had been fun for him to really let go and make a mess of things, but maybe now he was feeling that he shouldn't have done it, since he was so concerned about cleaning up.

C: I'm really messy, but I don't like to make messes.

T said that didn't make much sense to her.

He explained that he may leave things in a mess, then he feels bad when he comes back and sees it, and gets mad at himself for having done it.

T said maybe he's really afraid someone will get mad at him, or that he'll get punished for it. Then she tried to describe how he must feel inside when he's feeling guilty.

He agreed to all of this and smiled knowingly.

When T pointed out there were about five minutes left, he casually looked at the cookie jar. Then he played out one more sequence. The witch married the alligator. They got very hungry for real food but there wasn't any so the alligator had to eat the wastebasket, and the little toy clock "so they couldn't tell what time it is."

Has the mother at last but she deprives him of food. Doesn't want the hour to end

Then the alligator ate up the refrigerator "so if they did find some food there won't be any place to keep it." Finally they both starved to death.

Massive denial of oral pleasure (in presence of real food)

T said maybe he was really wanting to take some of the cookies, just like the witch and the alligator wanted real food, but maybe he was feeling uneasy about taking any.

He mumbled something about never really getting very hungry.

T assured him the cookies would always be there and he could have them if he wished.

Don then carefully replaced all the dollhouse furniture and put all the puppets back in their box. He left the room without taking any cookies.

NOTE: It appears that the alligator is going to be the main identification figure; with the witch, of course, serving as the bad mother. She does not provide adequate food, while the alligator demonstrates self-defeating tactics in eating up the refrigerator. All of this self-denial is in the presence of real cookies.

It may well be that the monkey and the "guest" who were responsible for so much of the changing of furniture represent the therapist who is ushering in changes.

Author's observations on second session. The second session extends and elaborates on the presenting problems. (Perhaps, for an obsessive–compulsive child, the ice can only be cracked in the first session.)

The witch puppet figures prominently as the controlling and orally depriving mother. She fights with other women to keep her man, and arranges the house so that cooking good meals is impossible.

The alligator (self figure?) is fed bad food that bites and stings his mouth. (Is this also a displacement from urethral to oral areas?) The chaotic and "messy" rearrangement of the bathroom furniture generates extreme anxiety as he hurries to put everything back in place. (His enuretic controls have been threatened.)

The therapist picks up on his initial ability to "let go and mess" and his subsequent feelings of concern. This discussion of his ambivalence leads to his admission of "feeling bad" (translate as feeling guilty) whenever he lets go spontaneously.

In the final oral–oedipal sequence, the witch (mother) and alligator (self) are married. The witch does not provide adequate food (affection). The alligator, starved for "real" food, engages in self-defeating masochistic maneuvers.

It may well be that the guest who was responsible for so much of the changing of furniture represents the therapist who is seen as ushering in changes.

In summary, this second session lays out Don's underlying problems in a manner more often seen in the initial session. In Don's case, the first session has demonstrated his usual and habitual manner of approach to situations, while the second session lays out virtually all of the suspected dynamic mechanisms that are basic to his symptoms.

Session 3

Don brought in a small orange plastic skeleton, which he said he got by trading one of his two plastic hot dogs to another boy. This skeleton was his identification figure throughout the session, and was eventually called "Skelly."

Sand was available for the first time today; he immediately expressed surprise and disgust, and "I bet the kids make a mess with that—making sand castles up to the ceiling." To T's pushing for his own reactions, he denied any personal feelings against dirt, just that it would be a lot of work for the janitors and they probably wouldn't like it.

Denial and distancing; takes vicarious pleasure in others' messiness and rationalizes his compulsiveness

T kept pointing out that he also probably didn't like the idea of dirt himself, and she continued such comments in subsequent play when he would be careful to brush off any loose sand from his hands and the cars he was playing with.

He used Skelly (SK) and the bicycle policeman (cyclist) for most of the hour, with many different sequences. In earlier ones, SK and the cyclist would go to the beach (sandtub). SK played tricks on people, changed their form; others wouldn't know it was he who was doing these things. "He's sneaky." There were car and cycle races, with SK usually winning. Once there was a fire and the fire engine was pressed into use. Don took the long white plastic tube (catheter?) which was the hose of the toy fire

Controls by being "sneaky," acts out through others

Reenacts early catheterizations with urethral-sexual connotations

engine and held it to the cycle, saying he was putting it into the hole of the gas tank, then "Phhhffff," there was an explosion.

The cyclist was changed by SK into an elephant and SK straddled its truck. The elephant wanted to be changed into a mouse, but had to remain an elephant. Then SK wanted to change him back into a cyclist but that seemed to be beyond his powers. So they both were to fight Bobo (a large inflated push toy). If the elephant won, he'd be changed back to the cyclist, but SK was not supposed to try *not* to win, or then the change could not take place. (In other words, SK's losing must be genuine.)

*Elephant =
father*

*Double bind;
must not
really
succeed*

So Don first had the elephant hit vigorously at Bobo, then SK hit very weakly. The puppets were asked to judge the winner, and selected the elephant, but they also said that SK was deliberately trying to be weak and stupid, so the elephant could not be changed back.

*Too danger-
ous to defeat
father; tries to
control by
playing dumb,
but can suc-
ceed when
puts forth real
effort*

T kept pointing out that SK seemed to be trying to be dumb, and to control grown-ups by acting stupid.

Then the elephant and SK had a direct fight; SK showed his real strength and won the bout, and the elephant was changed back into the cyclist, even though he lost.

T pointed out how proud SK must feel when he could show people how really good and strong he could be without having to pretend to be dumb.

The end of the bout was celebrated by Don giving each figure a piece of cookie, amid much exclamation about how good they were, and then popping them into his own mouth—his first attempt to eat.

Cannot eat directly; must disguise desires for oral gratification

The next sequence took place in the dollhouse which belonged to the General (father?). SK was told he could stay there. He would only do so on three conditions: (1) that he could have all the cookies he wanted; (2) that he could get up at midnight; (3) that he could have the house all to himself (thus getting rid of the father?). So the General went off to Honolulu.

Oedipal rivalry

SK and the cyclist got into bed together, with SK eating many cookies (Don actually doing so). SK was responsible for rearranging the house, removing the partitions so that the bedroom, bathroom, and kitchen furnishings were all available in the same room. SK got in the tub, still eating cookies. The cyclist asked for some and SK finally niggardly gave him a small piece which he crumbled up on the living room floor. SK asked the cyclist to clean up the floor, which the latter did by fooling SK and sweeping the crumbs under the bed. SK kept saying, "Um, um these cookies are good," until all were eaten (by Don!).

Pleasure in eating, but still vicariously

Denies oral pleasures to others

Insists on cleanliness from others but they can also be sneaky.

When told that five minutes remained, Don played out a final beach party in the sand. SK went on ahead of the cyclist and buried himself in the sand. The cyclist and other cars arrived, looked for SK, and finally uncovered him. SK said it wasn't so bad to be buried, it just feels like dirt on top of you. Then he said he was going to sleep for fifty years.

If buried can't be found or made to leave

T warned there was only one minute left.

Don held SK up in the air, saying "Mother Angel" up in the sky was calling SK to her for fifty years. SK said he didn't want to stay that long because his friend, the cyclist, would be too old when he returned. Mother and Father Angel said they could put a spell on the cyclist so he wouldn't age. Then SK flew back to earth, touched the cyclist, and said, "Goodbye, I'll see you in a couple of years," and then flew away. Then Don was ready to leave.

Must return to mother at end of session

Reluctant to go, but promises to return

Session 4

Don immediately related a scary dream, about a killer pushing against people with his whole body. He demonstrated by walking up to Bobo and doing the same. He said he doesn't watch the scary parts of TV shows; he closes his eyes but still listens.

Sex = aggression

He had brought a black plastic "Wolf-man" and built play sequences around it for most of the hour. First some dinosaur play, going back in time or into the future. Considerable time was spent in trying to defeat the rubber elephant who was the "Master," attacking him repeatedly on his trunk or using the trunk as a handle for overhead flips. There were karate fights, duels, and dart gun fights between the two. The Wolf-man finally won but was not satisfied!

Wolf-man = self

Oedipal rivalries

So next he fought the lion, who was King of the desert, and won, but again not satisfied. So he fought the President and the U.S. Army and won, so he was in control of America but this wasn't enough. Then he tackled the King of the World (the king puppet) and won this fight.

Son (Wolf-man) finally wins, but a hollow victory

None of his subjects would be friends with him; he tried various ways to win them over but with no success. Finally he got all the money in the world and divided it up among the people but they still didn't like him and wouldn't be friends. The Wolf-man felt so bad he finally killed himself.

Turns aggression inward and destroys self

A new sequence used the monkey puppets who were sick and given injections from the

Injections = probes

doctor kit. Then they needed glasses but they didn't like the red frames and wanted white instead. The grandfather monkey wanted to do something famous in order to get his name in the paper, but the most he could do was get in the comics.

Efforts to win attention are not successful, so reverts to sneaking and stealing

The final sequence was played out with the dollhouse dolls. They managed to end up with all the money in the world but couldn't decide how to use it, so they went out and stole the things they wanted.

(Throughout the session there was some talk of food and of being hungry, but Don did not eat any cookies today.)

Session 5

T asked Don some general questions about
school on the way to the playroom and commented on her first use of a "Do Not Disturb"
sign on the door. Don said his brother put up
such a sign on their bedroom door to keep out
their little brother. T encouraged more talk about
the big brother. Don gets most annoyed with him
over their go-cart, since his brother will use it for
half an hour, leaving only five minutes for Don.   *Represses an-*
Don doesn't dare show his anger.   *ger toward*
                                                     brother

   T reflected on how hard it must be to hold all
   the anger in, etc.

He sat a minute or two trying to decide what to   *Witch =*
do today. He had brought three small figures—   *mother*
the two previous ones (Skelly and Wolf-man)
and an old witch. Then he launched into a
thirty-five to forty-minute sequence with the   *His own*
witch and her two sons. She was 355 years old,   *mother*
and kept having babies and finally she died. She   *has had*
had told her sons of three enemies she had, so   *miscarriages–*
they set out to eliminate them: another old witch   *does he fear*
who was 500 years old, dinosaurs, and the   *she would*
policeman. The sons found the first two and   *die?*
killed them off.
   This was all quite coherent, but when it came   *Policeman*
to fighting the policeman (motorcycle cop), the   *continues to*
play broke down and he never quite got to this   *be father—*
figure. After several abortive maneuvers he set   *rival, whom*

up six or eight of the plastic soldiers and defeated them, calling one of them the policeman.

    he doesn't dare defeat

Now the witch–mother could come back to life, and this was followed by several instances of her having a baby and either she or her sons expressing fears that she would die.

    Again, fears for mother and her pregnancies

T kept reflecting on how children are afraid their mothers might die when they have babies, it's a pretty awful feeling, etc. (as this play was obviously dealing with his own mother's miscarriages).

Then the alligator puppet was introduced as a child the witch had had long ago, but who now had grown up. This creature was a weakling and cried easily. The alligator and the other two "sons" got hungry. The witch–mother only gave them a half cookie apiece (here he started eating the cookies he used in the play), then the alligator left to find food for himself.

    Alligator = self figure

    Mother is stingy and withholding

T commented on the stingy mother who won't let her children have all the food and goodies they want.

The alligator came back to report he had eaten the General's car; then the elephant appeared as the General in new form. The Wolf-Man used all kinds of karate tricks and finally got rid of the elephant, so the sons have the mother all to themselves.

    Oedipal rivalries eliminate the father, so sons have mother alone

There were more episodes of the witch–mother not feeding the sons, and leaving home but returning.Finally both sons died and the mother had two new sons, they died and were revived over and over. Finally he put all three figures in his pocket, as if to end the series.

Mother is orally depriving; sons can never please her (or reenacts births and miscarriages)

T called attention to the fact that only five minutes remained. This stimulated quite an episode of eating cookies, via the elephant and the camel, who were in a zoo, and kept saying, "Oh, such good cookies," while Don ate them. Then the animals went to the circus, but were only given water there, and so they went back to the zoo.

Pleasure in oral gratification, but still through proxies

T kept reflecting on how good it is to have all they want in the zoo.

Zoo = therapy; circus = home and mother

The elephant left to find some peanuts and the camel hurried to eat all the rest of the cookies so there would be none left for the elephant.

Sibling rivalry

T commented that he wants them all to himself; he doesn't want to have to share these good things.

The camel grew old, feeble, and weak-legged, but still kept eating.

T: Even if he's crippled and stupid, people still like him and give him all he wants. It's nice to know he can have all of this.

Finally, all the real cookies were consumed. The
camel left and went to the desert and fell on his
side where the elephant found him. The camel
died, as the time was up.

*It's dangerous
to satisfy
desires*

Session 6

When Don first sat down at the table he saw the
new water pistol. (The previous one had been
broken since Don had begun therapy.) T commented that this one looked like it would really
work and asked if he had one of his own. Don
told of a time when he was shooting with one
into a cup, and another boy ran across the line of
fire and got wet. The next day he got Don wet.

*Friend "acci-
dentally" gets
wet. Denies
any aggres-
sive feelings*

T talked about maybe he was a little glad he
got the boy, but he kept denying this. Finally
he admitted it had been a little "funny."

Then he got the dart guns and spent the entire
hour with them. First he used the target, often
hitting the 500 and 1000 rings, and looking quite
pleased with himself.

*Some feelings
of competence*

T commented on his good feelings when he is
successful.

Then he lined up animals on the table (choosing
the elephant first, then a lion, wolf, etc.). He
tried first to hit the elephant but was unable to
topple it.

*Oedipal ri-
valry again*

T kept commenting on its being so big, the
boss, and it had been the general last week;
now he was trying to see if he really could get
the better of him.

He shot and knocked over all the other animals
but never could get the elephant. (Actually it is

too big and solid for success to be possible.) But he was pleased with his other successes and became more and more animated as T cheered him on. Finally he said, "This is fun!" Then he set up rows of animals without the elephant. Once, as he reached for a dart, his hand went near and over the cookie jar, "Oh, I almost took a cookie."

T reassured him that he could have all he wanted.

Soon he started reaching for, and eating, a cookie whenever he missed a shot (only three altogether). After the animals, he set up a row of rubber soldiers and had more success in getting each of these each time, becoming quite excited and interested in the game.

First direct eating of cookies; uses as a comforting device

When told there were just two minutes left, he set up just a single soldier on the table and shot it; then set it on the floor, so it would be more difficult to get at; then lay on the floor himself and took aim but missed. Then he stood up and closed his eyes to shoot and missed again. Finally, he shot it with his eyes open and got it.

Too threatening to shoot father figure directly

T kept reflecting through all of this how he seemed to want to shoot the one most important soldier, yet he was making it impossible for himself to do it.

In the course of this session Don got the knees of his pants quite dusty. Toward the end of

Compulsive concern

the hour, he had begun brushing them off. T asked if he were afraid his mother would scold. He said she would only if she thought he had tried to get himself dirty. Just before going out the door, he gave them one final brushing.

T said she guessed he really did seem worried about it.

Session 7

Don couldn't decide what to do at first, then settled on the soldiers which he set up to shoot, because they were "easier than the animals." After one round he changed to the animals. At first he said he would leave out the elephant, then changed his mind.

Indecisive

While shooting he talked about the hunting trip with his family this past weekend. He had shot a rifle and the BB gun, but he was only allowed to go out for one half-day while his brother went each day. Don would be promised each time that he could go too, but then was not taken. T asked who had promised; he said his father.

Each time that T would reflect on his disappointments and the angry feelings he must have had, he would say, "Yes, but . . . not enough room," or some other adult "decided to go at the last minute," etc. T kept emphasizing that even though there were good reasons he still must have felt pretty bad.

Makes excuses and rationalizes

Real trouble admitting to any hostile feelings

He is to get his own BB gun on his ninth birthday, just as Joe got his. At first he was to get Joe's hand-me-down, but Joe is still not old enough to have a real gun, so Don will get his own gun. Since his birthday is Christmas Eve he is not expecting toys, just parts for his bike.

Doesn't really expect to have anything of his own

He played out a sequence with the motorcycle

cop and the fire-chief car. They were in two
stations side by side. When the buildings were
enlarged, they touched each other, so no one *Identity issues*
knew where one building left off and the other
began. Then the officers started doing each
other's jobs, but then would be scolded by their
chiefs; for example, the cop started putting out
fires. One time when he was putting out a little
fire, it started raining so hard it not only put out
the fire, but softened the ground so that the cop
and his motorcycle sank in the ground (the sand
box) until only his head was showing. The fire
chief came along and thought it was a statue. The
cop finally got out and had to confess he was
putting out fires. Don then picked up the motor- *Bedwetting*
cycle to put it away, brushed off the wet sand, *and/or mas-*
then took it to the sink to wash it off. *turbation guilt*

T asked if he was upset by the dirt because he
was afraid he might be scolded, or because he
really didn't like to have things dirty. He
denied both and said he was thinking what the
other kids would feel and say, "ugh," etc. if
the toys were dirty. T also asked if he were
wondering about the other children who came
here; he said he knew others did come. T
explained that others came, and that other
people saw kids as well as herself.

Then the big (green) and little (red) racers had *Identifies with*
a race around the outside of the sand tub. The *father; wants*
green one won. Then the next race was won by *to be big and*
the red (small) racer who got a cookie as the *win, but feels*
prize (which Don ate). Then the little red car *inadequate*

thought that if he put on the wheels from the big
racer he could go even faster. (Don's father drag
races!) So he put the wheels of the green racer on
the little car, but they soon fell off.

T said it looked like the little car wanted to
have the big wheels and everything else the big
car had.

For the next race each car had a pusher; the
little red racer had a big red car, and the big
green racer had a little green car. The racers each
got stuck so the pushers carried on the race, with
the big pusher winning for the little car and
receiving a cookie for the trophy–reward.

Indirectly triumphs over father

Then Don drew a picture of a racing car, with
a huge driver sticking out of the top (with a big
head, racing cap, dark-glass goggles, mustache,
and beard). A bare foot protrudes under the car,
and a long arm reaches out to clasp the trunk of
a tree which the car is crashing into. The fingers
are touching a hole in the trunk, steam is coming
out of the radiator under the arm, and mice are
coming out of a suitcase at the rear of the car.
(This all looked pretty masturbatory.)

Masturbatory symbolism

Babies?

T kept commenting on the driver holding the
trunk, how it just fits his hands, he could get
his fingers all around it to hold on, etc.

Then he added a witch, with a long crooked
nose and broomstick, behind the racer; and a bat,
with outstretched wings, in front and above the
car.

Racer = self (or father)
Witch = mother

Bat = father?

Session 8

Don stood around at first, couldn't decide   *Indecisive*
whether to play or draw; finally decided to draw,
using the Bobo as a model. In reaching for the
crayons he "accidentally" put his hand in the   *Hides desire*
cookie jar and said, "Oops, the wrong thing." T   *for food, with*
encouraged him to take some, but he didn't until   *self-denial*
later in the hour.   *taking over*

While drawing he said this was one thing he
could do better than his brother.

T commented it seemed that in most things he
felt he couldn't do as well as his brother, or
didn't get to do as much—like on the hunting
trip. Immediately there were denials and
excuses—his brother already had a real gun so   *Denial and*
he should get to go more. T kept emphasizing   *rationalization*
that he always was giving reasons but she
guessed he really did feel bad and disappointed
lots of the time. There was very little acknowl-
edgment from Don.

He drew a large Bobo face, omitting the red
nose until last and said it really wouldn't be that
color. He added stars and a quarter-moon around   *Avoids and*
the head. He turned the paper over and drew the   *denies redness*
small bear named Booboo that is painted on the
back of the Bobo toy. Then he printed the names
of each figure, getting too many o's in Bobo, so
that it also read as Booboo; he said he made a
"booboo." He tried drawing a helicopter without   *Feels*
a model, getting disgusted with his effort and   *inadequate*
quit.

He got out the puppets, the skunk and cat, and took them to the dollhouse. The cat owned the house and wouldn't let the skunk come in. This was reenacted with the dog and skunk. Then the alligator owned the house and the skunk would sneak in without being noticed. The skunk would upset all the furniture and eat all the cookies (Don was really gulping them for the skunk). The alligator finally woke up and was very cross, especially because the food was gone. Finally the alligator agreed to let the skunk stay and sleep on the couch.

Vicarious pleasure in anality and naughtiness

T's comments during the eating sequence were directed toward the stinginess of the alligator, and its not wanting to feed others.

Oral indul-gence is not approved by parental figures

Session 9

Don used the sand tub, smoothing out all the sand, then lining the trucks all around the edge with two cars, the generals, in the middle. The trucks attacked first, but all were demolished. In the second set-up one car, not a general, survived.

Attacks the General and succeeds

    T kept talking about them all wanting to get rid of the two big bosses, and Don smiled as he continued the play.

He was somewhat upset by all the wet sand that stuck to the cars but, nevertheless, he did not wipe them off as he put them back on the shelf, only shook each one.

Can accept some messiness now

    He very briefly reached for the water pistol, shook his head, and started to leave that shelf.

    T asked if he didn't really want to use it, and he started giving excuses, how he could have as much fun shooting without getting things wet. T recalled other times when he had made excuses to hide what he really wanted to do.

Self-denial and excuses again

Then he did go back and load the water gun. He laid out a plastic paint smock on the table, even though T kept reassuring him that water couldn't hurt anything in the playroom. He set up series of toy soldiers, dinosaurs, large and small animals, and shot them down. He showed more

Overcomes his reluctance but still can't be really free and spontaneous

delight than usual for him, when he would get them all, or a particularly difficult shot. When he was through he wiped the water off the table and wall.

T kept saying that he didn't need to do this, that water wouldn't hurt anything, and that this must seem a strange place where he could do things like that and not get scolded.

With only five minutes left, he brought the domestic animals to the table and set them up on two sides, the good and the bad. They attacked each other, particularly trying to get the bull which eventually fell. When it was time to go he carefully set them up on a different shelf, so he could have them next time.

Freedom of playroom versus parental restrictions

T reminded him that other children use the room and she couldn't promise that the animals would still be in the same place next week, because other doctors and children also use the room all week. He said he knew this; that was all right. T commented that at least this way he could tell if other kids really had come in.

Session 10

The little animals were on the same shelf where he had left them last time. He went right to them and brought them to the sand tub. He laid out several different farm scenes in the sand, smoothing out pens, making hills, a mud hole for the pigs to lie in, a pond for the ducks, and separate fields for each species of animal. He added a strip of wood for a feed trough but never had the animals eat. He placed a chicken on a ridge so it could watch all the other animals; later one of the farmers was located so he could keep track of everybody. Then a bomb came through and destroyed everything. Even in death each type of animal was buried in its special place separate from the others. In the final sequence, the farmer only allowed a very small space for all the animals, so that they were all crowded together with only standing room. Then Don lined them all up on the table from the biggest to the smallest, then put them all carefully back on the shelf.

Very controlled and contained, but allows pigs a special place to be messy

"Children" are closely supervised and restricted

Compulsive

Then he used the dart guns, shooting at the motorcycle cop and getting it on the first round. He said that was too easy. He then set up the baby bottle (the first time he has touched it) but that was also too easy a target. He spent some time trying to hit the lion and finally succeeded.

Is this a wish to regress?

T reflected that he seemed to be wanting something hard to do, and feels good when he succeeds.

Don brought out two rubber knives. He then laid the two sand scoops end-to-end in the sand and put a small toy boat at one end (for the apple on the figure's head). First he dropped the knives on the "head" repeatedly, then deliberately aimed for the joining of the two scoops (groin area).

Castration fantasy

T said it looked like he was trying to get him in the middle where it really hurts.

The boat then became a person, with a long sequence of hiding it under mounds of sand and jabbing at it as a magician does in cutting through boxes to divide a person. Soon the magician aspect was dropped and he was making direct jabs, sometimes with his eyes closed. Throughout, he was quite intent on hitting the mark.

Is the aggressor, but at first had to do it under the guise of a magician

T commented he was trying to be sure to get him in certain places; there must be lots of blood and gore; where did it get him—his arms, legs, middle, bottom? In answer to the latter questions he thought a moment and said, "The middle." While he kept hitting harder and harder, T wondered how "he" (the person figure) must feel, it must be awful to not know when and where you're going to be hurt.

Reliving the intrusive procedures of his infancy traumas

He agreed to all of this and that it would hurt. Then he put a sand scoop over the boat (person) as a shield; finally he removed the boat and jabbed at the scoop. (By this point he seemed to be getting considerable satisfaction out of being the aggressor, rather than identifying with the victim.)

NOTE: Is some guilt also being expressed here in connection with mother's frequent miscarriages; the fear that he may have pushed her in the stomach, and been responsible?

Session 11

Most of the session was spent with small animals in the sand tub, with the bull terrorizing the other animals. Once he put several small animals in the baby carriage from the dollhouse. This particularly angered the bull and he charged into the carriage and was generally destructive.

As he left the session he said, "That was all because of the bull."

NOTE: A much less active session than the last one, with fewer changes of "props." Is this a retreat from all of his exposure last time? Or placing the "blame" where it belongs, on the father?

Bull = a father who dislikes babies

Was father responsible for the miscarriages?

Session 12

Don was very noncommittal in response to T's
inquiries as to how he had spent his Thanksgiv-
ing vacation. He said he had played some with
an older boy, who is older than his brother, and
who also has a brother a little younger than Don.

He went to the sand and set up a sequence
involving a rich man who had a vehicle that
acted like a rocket in the air, but it could also go   *Masturbatory*
underwater with the help of retractable wings.   *fantasy*
The rocket flew in the air and then the pilot
forgot to punch the button to let the wing out
when he hit the water. The pilot and the rich man
were sent to jail for fooling all the people and for
accumulating large debts in constructing the
machine.

In the next sequence a poor man was intro-   *Identity*
duced. The rich man got to the bank first,   *confusions*
pretending he was the poor man and tried to take
what little money he (the poor man) had from the
bank, but the banker recognized him and
wouldn't give him the money. When the poor
man got to the bank the banker thought it was the
rich man again and so wouldn't give him his own
money. Both men ended in jail.

In both sequences T kept commenting that
people were pretending to be somebody else,
or to do something that couldn't be done.

In a new sequence a horse was approached
by a small duck who asked to ride on his back.

The horse agreed, and also let a little chicken get on his back for a ride. Then a man figure arrived and asked to get on, but the duck and chicken didn't want him, so a fight ensued.

T reflected that it looked like the kids didn't want the father around. Don looked very thoughtful, said nothing, but took the animals back to the shelf and brought over a collection of dinosaurs and fish.

Play disruption (T probably pushed too soon here)

In the dinosaur–fish play there was much discussion between the fish, who were living on land, and the dinosaurs, who were in the water.

Reversal of roles, or identity confusion

Here T summarized the play to this point—it seemed that in each play today people were not recognized for what they really were; maybe just like sometimes girls wish they were boys, or boys wish they were girls; or maybe sometimes people call boys "sissies" but they know they're still boys. Don kept his back to T all this time, seemed thoughtful, and nodded very slightly.

Then he added an Indian figure and little plastic spears. The dinosaurs weren't sure this was really an Indian until he had done much jabbing of the fish and dinosaurs. Then there was a final battle between the Indian and a very bull-like dinosaur with sharp horns.

Must prove his manliness

Then Don got the two rubber knives and the boat (which he had used two weeks before) and said, "I'm going to play with the knives again."

He buried the boat in the sand and kept sticking the knives in with much realistic grimacing, jabbing again and again.

T asked if he had ever been cut with knives. As usual he denied any hurts but discussed in great detail all the hurts of his brother, such as hitting his head on rocks, ice, and steps. T asked how he felt when he saw blood on his brother. He said he didn't like it, but that he didn't usually see the blood; once he'd come in and seen his brother's dirty shirt. T kept pointing out how he always denies unpleasant things and his not wanting to talk about such things. Finally, he said he once had cut his leg and had a scar he'd have for the rest of his life. T again pointed out how he had been denying by talking only about his brother's hurts. She guessed he really did find it hard to talk about these things.

Denials, as usual, but finally admits

Don noticed a new, shorter dart gun on the shelf, but said he didn't think there was time to use it (although he knew there were still five minutes left). T said he could do a lot in five minutes, so then he did use it. Then he washed the sand off his hands before leaving. (This is the first he had gone to the sink to wash his own hands directly—previously it's been via the toys.)

Uses excuses for self-denial

Session 13

Don brought a green plastic figure that looked like a robed priest, whom he called a magician. This figure went through some magic sequences, showing others how he could jump from a hill and stop himself in midair. The action finally developed with the figure not liking to be called "weakling," "shorty," "ugly," and "sissy" (after T added this in repeating the list). In turn, different cars would come up the hill; the figure would shoot at them or upturn the car to show his strength—all the while shouting and defying them to call him these names. Finally the "others" accepted him into their group and even went out of their way to fix up a stage and props so the figure could give his magic shows.

Reenacting conflicts with brother and peers; probably has been called all of these names

All this time T kept reflecting in terms of this figure wanting to show folks how big and strong he really was, wanting to be accepted and not to be called names, and how glad he was when finally accepted.

Then there was a brief sequence with the priest–magician figure in the dollhouse, wanting to find someone his own size, objecting to there being seven babies (all the dollhouse dolls). Finally the family kept increasing to twenty-one, and the figure "gave up."

Then Don started shooting darts at a new Bobo, first aiming for his hat, then the nose. Then he had the robed figure hit at Bobo. For the last ten minutes of the hour, Don was hitting Bobo directly (for the first time), giving him

Drops symbolic, proxy attacks and goes at Bobo directly

vigorous beatings, twisting, tossing, kicking, and hitting him in the mouth, nose, stomach, and small of the back. During all of this, he talked to T about their big shepherd dog, saying he wasn't afraid of it; then saying it was like a wrestling match to play with it; and that he didn't want to go into the garage for his bike if the dog was nearby.

T kept trying to help him to describe his fearfulness and to recognize these feelings. He kept denying any fear, but would admit he did get a "funny feeling."

Denies, then admits, his fears

Then, while holding the plastic figure to beat Bobo, he started saying, "Don't you call me a sissy," as he would alternately hit weakly and strongly, with the figure held out to do the hitting.

T: "You'll show them now how strong you really are," etc. Once he addressed T directly saying: "If this was my brother . . . oh, boy!" and T talked about his wishing to get the better of him and be stronger.

Brother is now the antagonist, and he really gives it to him!

He continued this very strong Bobo beating until the hour was up. Then he hauled off with one last strong punch, saying, "See *you* next week."

Session 14

Since there were only twelve days until Christmas, T talked about the trees in the clinic, and had his family decorated theirs yet. He reported that his father said that two weeks was enough, one week before Christmas and one after.

T asked how he felt; would he like it up longer? Again he started rationalizing that the baby brother would have it pretty well messed up if it were up too long. T observed that she thought he really would like it up longer.

Rationalizes any negative feelings toward father

The entire hour was spent with Bobo one way or another. First he spent fifteen minutes with very hard hits and punches, karate thrusts, and tossing and throwing it across the room. Then he put objects on Bobo's head, à la William Tell, and shot at these with the dart gun. Next he drew the face of Bobo on the painting easel; then, as he hit him in the eye, he'd blacken the pictured eye. He did the same for the mouth, with some "blood dripping," but when he hit the nose, he drew an X over the nose in the picture.

Direct expression of aggression

Mentions blood on picture of Bobo

T commented on the blood; how did he feel about blood?

There was not much response at the moment, but very soon he was choking and "strangling" Bobo. With more direct punches he volunteered

Finally can relate to own experience

that he had frequent nosebleeds; in fact, he'd had one the week before. If they're not too bad he takes care of them himself; they usually happen when he's in bed.

T encouraged more discussion, and suggested maybe he's afraid he'll get a bloody nose if he fights other fellows. C: "The easiest way to get one (nosebleed) is to lie down."

Passive submission

He started jabbing Bobo with the rubber knives, but this seemed too threatening, so he got out the doctor kit, put different objects on Bobo's head, glasses on his nose, the syringe on his head, saying he was getting him ready for an operation. He pretended to shave Bobo by scraping a knife across his face. He kept talking about the operation, holding his hands up like a doctor getting ready to scrub up, even going into the lavatory and turning on the water. He never did go through with the operation. Instead he filled the water pistol and said he would "finish him off" that way. He did shoot considerable water at it. When told there were three or four minutes left, he announced there would be five more big punches and two twists, which he did, and then one tremendous final blow.

Can't quite use knives on Bobo

Masquerades aggression as an operation, but can't carry through with it

Cathartic session with direct expression of aggressive feelings

Session 15

Don started in on Bobo at once, harder than previously, and for most of the hour. He aimed especially at Bobo's nose and was happy when it would get bashed in. Once he started to wipe "his bloody nose" with his tie, but quickly dropped this. He strangled Bobo with the jump-rope; once he called Bobo a baby while tossing the toy around and then putting it upside down in the wastebasket.

Real catharsis via direct action

Still skittish about blood

Then he set up contests (where he took both sides) putting snakes on Bobo's head and shooting them off; then shooting at cars to see how far they would go. Then each contestant tried to see who could break a plastic jar lid. (He was very careful to pick up all the pieces and put them in the wastebasket.) Once he "killed" Bobo, then immediately gave him a lot of toy money.

Restitution

T reflected he must feel guilty and had to make up to him.

Another time he got out the stethoscope to see if Bobo were still alive. Shortly before the end of the hour he dropped these contests and set up situations where he would compete against his own previous records, leaving the Bobo play and trying to roll cars through smaller and smaller openings in a block wall he set up at the other end of the room.

Enjoys challenges.

Session 16

When T asked how his Christmas was, Don said, "Not so good." He then spent much of the hour discussing the death of his dog. Also one of the neighborhood boys had stolen money and a minibike from Don's family and had been picked up by the police. His mother seemed to miss the dog almost more than the children did and was already talking about replacing it. Don was really quite unhappy also.

Serious discussion

As for the neighbor boy, Don's mother had only warned him when he took $3 from them; now father says she should have reported this to the police which might have prevented the bigger theft. Don kept repeating what he had probably heard the parents say over and over, "I guess he thought if he could get away with the money he could also get away with stealing the bike." The boy's name is Joe—the same as Don's big brother, and he completely blocked on the last name. They all had to go down to the police station to claim the bike.

At this point he excused himself to go to the bathroom—the only time he has had to go during a session.

When he returned T talked about his feelings through all the bike trouble; and was he afraid at the police station? He immediately said, "No" but his little brother (age two) was, because his mother kept telling him that if he wasn't good he'd have to stay in jail. Don

Initial denial of feelings; discusses in terms of little brother then

commented he didn't think his brother was old enough to know what this really meant. T kept pressuring him about his own feelings, and he admitted he did feel a little funny. T reminded him that he seems to always deny his own fears and will start talking about someone else's. He then said he wasn't afraid but he did feel nervous and he guessed that was a kind of fear.

finally admits to his own

His big Christmas present was a walkie-talkie. "It cost about $30. Joe also got one so our folks must have spent about $50. You have to have two in order to use either one." Joe sneaks Don's out to use with his friends but gets mad whenever Don asks to use his.

His birthday was Christmas Eve but he elected not to celebrate it yet—last year he waited and had it in March with his father. He brought up the topic of the birthday card T had sent him, laughed and tried to repeat the jingle, then reached into his pocket for the card, but decided he had forgotten and left it at school.

He took a cookie, then got out the small cars and played out a sequence of a boy getting caught for some misdemeanor and saying he was the sergeant's son.

T tried to draw comparisons with the actual event of the neighbor boy who was caught and was from a family where you wouldn't expect this sort of thing. He denied the similarity, saying the boy wasn't really the sergeant's son; he had just said he was. He was able to

Can't yet take such obvious parallels

accept T's further discussion that he must find it
hard to realize that someone he knew and
thought was good could really do these things.

Resents
authority
figures

The next sequence was of army privates in a
truck giving a show for the President and the
General who were in two small cars. It ended
with the privates blowing up the cars.

He selected the box of toy money from the
cupboard and told of playing with a lot at his
cousin's. They just threw up handfuls of it. He
did the same here and was quite lively, free, and
relaxed. When asked what he would do with so
much money if it were real, he had very little to
offer, except that he would save most of it.

He then looked around to see if he could find
something he had never played with before, but
couldn't, so he picked the wild animals. Generally, they all ate each other up, with only the
elephant remaining. Don said the giraffe was the
one in real trouble because he has no way to
defend himself except to run.

In a final puppet scene, the devil asked for the
King, but was told the Queen was the most
powerful. The witch arrived and threatened the
devil, so the devil lunged toward her—horns
foremost. The witch put a spell on him and   *Castrating*
changed him into a little girl with the King and   *females*
Queen watching all of this.

T commented that both women (Queen and
witch) seemed stronger than the men; they
were the bosses.

Session 17

Don spent the first thirty minutes in brutal beating of Bobo, swinging, punching, and throwing it against chairs and under the easel. Once he mumbled something about "my friends" (but nothing more was audible). Then he stood over Bobo and pushed his arm down inside the head and body, and said, "Now your mother won't know you."

Much release of hostility

T reflected in terms of lots of changes taking place.

Bobo is his "old" self he wants to get rid of, but Mother may not be liking the change

He went to the easel and drew spots for his and Bobo's locations in two opposite corners of the room, then a jerky line to indicate his advance toward Bobo, two smudges where they met and fought, then a coffin for Bobo. Then he reenacted all this for real, burial and all.

T's comments included pointing out that he felt he had to give fair warning before killing Bobo.

Later, he threatened to eat Bobo, glaring down at him with bared teeth. Then he brought over a cup and plate, knife, fork, and spoon, "cut out a slice" of Bobo and went through the motions of eating, saying it tasted horrible.

Orally aggressive

Puppet sequences used the skunk and a variety of the furry animals. The skunk's house (dollhouse) was dirty and he asked different animals to clean it for him, but each of them refused, even for pay. Then the skunk offered a steak to the dog; the dog didn't do a good enough job, but finally got the steak anyway. Then the alligator was hired and did a good job. While the skunk was praising him, the radio came on and announced that everyone should look out for the alligator because it had just eaten two people. When the skunk accused the alligator, the alligator ate the skunk also. This ended that play.

T pointed out the similarity to his thinking the neighbor boy was good, then finding out that he was wanted by the police. He seemed rather taken aback and was silent. T then asked if anything new had developed this past week, but he said he had not seen the boy.

Can't tolerate interpretations too "close to home"

Don noticed that only five minutes remained and took a cookie saying, "One for the road" and laughed as he ate it.

Uncomfortable, wants session to end; or to tide himself over until next session

He set up the dollhouse dolls and rearranged all the furniture, with mother at the sink, the children in bed or on the toilet, and father on the couch complaining that he wanted the house clean. Mother also didn't like to see the kids sneaking cookies.

Freer use of cookies, in spite of mother's restrictions

When T inquired if that was also true at home, he admitted his mother was that way too.

When it was time to go he took another cookie. When T said, "One for the road," he smiled and left in a happy mood.

Session 18

T was a few minutes late picking him up in the
waiting room; he was looking around the corner
for her.

 T discussed his probable uneasiness, but he
denied being upset.

*Anxious and
uneasy when
T is late*

He went first for Bobo and there was much
throwing over his shoulder and pounding it on
the floor. Once he said, "Oh, if he were real!"

*Is moving
from symbol
to reality and
can verbalize
feelings
directly*

With T's help he was able to talk about how he
would like to be able to show a friend of his
that he could stand up for himself "a little, but
not enough that he would no longer be
friends."

Bobo eventually started leaking sand from its
base but Don didn't seem too upset. Nevertheless he kept commenting on it.

 He was able to accept T's explanation that lots
of children use Bobo and he just happened to
be the last one to use it as it was splitting apart.
Then he volunteered that he knew he couldn't
be the only child coming and using the room,
they wouldn't be able to keep up a room for
just one child. This led into a discussion of
how he felt about T seeing other children, and
didn't he sometimes wish that he was the only
one? He denied this, and said he wouldn't care
if he saw first one person, then another, and
back to the first, just so he saw somebody.
During this discussion the ball he was tossing

*Denies possi-
ble jealousy
and "turns
tables" to not
caring if he
see another
therapist*

about came close to T and he was somewhat
alarmed.

He looked in the cupboard to see if there was
anything he hadn't played with before, saying he
used to use darts each time. He did find a new
small-size Slinky. This elicited much exploration
and play, especially in seeing how long it could
be stretched. He blew up a balloon and tried to
push it through the outstretched Slinky. Then he
ate a cookie.

Feels freer to reach out and explore

Relives urethral probes

The rest of the hour was spent with the
balloons, selecting only the long ones from the
box of long and round. He tried to tie one on
Bobo's nose but that didn't work. He blew them
up, inserting darts in the ends, and let them go,
hoping they would gradually lose air. Then he
filled balloons with water, saying they looked
like baby bottles, then held them up so that they
looked saggy. He talked to the balloons under his
breath while at the sink.

Much phallic symbolism and refers to earlier urethral trauma

T said he would probably like to drop these
water balloons on the floor and see the splash.

He did drop some in the sink. He was thoroughly
enjoying all of this and was jolly and animated.
He laid a blown-up balloon in the sand tub and
jabbed at it with a rubber knife until it burst,
saying this was an "operation." (T did not learn
until later that he had been told that warts were
soon to be removed from his feet.) He put three

Getting closer to feeling comfortable with possibility of messing balloons in his mouth at once, blowing them up slightly, saying they were cigars.

*Are append-
ages today
phallic or
wart symbols?*

    T talked about his many interests today in the long things, and things that stick out.

He blew up a balloon and clipped it onto the easel so that it stuck up and out; then he shot at it with darts from which he had removed the rubber tips. Then he jabbed at it with the knife saying, quite spontaneously, "Now I'm *really* mad," and continued jabbing until it burst.

*Can express
anger verbally*

    It was then time to leave. He started for the door then turned back with an "Uh, uh" and reached for a cookie, started to leave again then went back for a second one.

*Seeks comfort
in cookies*

    T said, "You need to take enough to keep you going until next time" and he smiled assent.

Interim Progress Report

Report on the first four months of therapy; a total of eighteen sessions.

Don was eight years, nine months of age when therapy was begun, and was repeating second grade. Referral problems included poor schoolwork in spite of better-than-average intellectual ability, feelings of inadequacy, and many fears of blood, pain, and bodily injuries. He was reported to have frequent nosebleeds and to have been much concerned over his mother's miscarriages.

Don's early behavior in the therapy hours is best described in terms of the progress so far. At first he was very precise, controlled, and methodical in everything he did. He would decide what he was going to use, set up routines for play, and was careful to replace objects precisely where they had been, and to clean up any mess, such as sand, which might have spilled. He has now explored all the toys in the room and, in fact, indicates some boredom because there is nothing new. He now can tolerate messes of water or sand, makes little move to clean off the toys, and seems to be building up to really messing or splashing.

He has moved from little or no expressions of affect, even when encouraged by the therapist, to being able to acknowledge feelings of pleasure when successful and anger when mad. A few times he has spontaneously made such statements as "Now I'm really mad" (at Bobo), or "This is fun." Initially, when confronted with affect-laden experiences, he would deny his feelings, either rationalizing and excusing or ascribing them to others. This was true in a variety of areas, such as feelings about dirt and messing, hunger, pain and hurts, blood, anger, fears, and any desires for toys or his fair share of attention and privileges. Now, with help, he can admit to some of these, and accept the therapist's interpretations of how he must be feeling.

As an example of his constriction, during the first session in which he gave any indication of seeing the cookies he played out a sequence (with the puppets) of animals being starved, but he did not take any of the real food. The next session, again in the toy play, he gave bits of cookies to the toy soldiers, then ate these himself almost as a way of getting rid of the "props." His first direct eating occurred in the sixth session, when he would help himself, and eat directly, whenever he missed a shot with the darts. Lately, he quite openly helps himself to one or two as he is leaving, which the therapist has interpreted to him as wanting something to keep him going until next time.

The first twelve sessions were largely spent in acting out numerous play sequences with puppets, soldiers, cars, trucks, and rubber animals. He accompanies the play with verbal running accounts demonstrating an active, free-flowing, and unself-conscious fantasy. Themes have included animals and people changing form and species; food deprivations by women; control over men exercised largely by the witch; the owner of a house hiring persons to clean and never being satisfied (this latter is usually followed by scenes of somebody sneaking into the house, completely upsetting all the furniture, and eating all the food); self-defeating maneuvers (e.g., you will win only if you lose, but you must not try to lose); many oedipal rivalries involving pitting strength against a general, a monster, or the president.

These oedipal sequences have gradually been replaced by concerns with identity (people pretending to be someone else); this led to portrayal of the figures being called weakling and sissy; and from there the symbolism has been more in terms of efforts to be accepted by his peers and, probably, his big brother. This shift was revealed through his progressive use of Bobo. At first he would only attack it through other small objects held in his hand or by shooting at it with darts. During the 13th session, following his play with doll figures, in which one was called ugly and weak, he started for Bobo directly with his fists and has continued very vigorous pummeling ever since. He has been much more relaxed and freer in his conversation and activities since this quite evident catharsis. He also now refers to Bobo in terms of wishing he could do as much to his brother or his friends. There has also been some suggestion that he is aware mother may not approve of increased aggression.

At deeper levels, some of the play symbolism has indicated strong guilt feelings, the need for punishment or restitution, masturbatory impulses, and considerable preoccupation with working through the trauma of the urethral probes in early infancy, as he pushes darts and rubber tubes into small openings and jabs knives into balloons or objects hidden in the sand. (These latter activities possibly may also refer to guilt and fears concerning any responsibility he may feel for his mother's miscarriages.) He has finally been able to discuss his own nosebleeds, but only after several sessions of denial or attributing such happenings to his brother or to Bobo.

There certainly has been progress in his ability to handle and express threatening impulses directly which, in turn, has resulted in a much freer and spontaneous general attitude on his part. He still cannot accept interpretations of his play themes which are too direct or which relate play events to real-life experiences. It is also noteworthy that this boy has never once attempted to test the limits; at no time has he done anything that would require a limit to be set. So far, any feelings about his mother and father have been revealed only through symbolic figures; there has been very little play with, or reference to, human parents, although he is beginning to use the family dollhouse dolls rather than concentrating on the animals and puppets.

Process Notes, Sessions 19–32

Session 19

NOTE: Don's father came in today to join his mother in her usual session with her therapist.

Don started talking about Cub Scouts and that his mother is the den mother. At the last pack meeting Don got up to the final round in their car races, pitted against a boy named Joe (his brother's name!). The other boy won but Don was able to express considerable pride, as well as surprise, that he had done as well as he did.

Takes pride in accomplishments

He was reluctant to hit Bobo very hard, because he was afraid the new patch might come off, so he ended up throwing darts and the ball at it instead. He also threw the ball at the ceiling, aiming once as if he were going to throw it at the light, but quickly backed off.

First tentative testing of limits

T reflected his urge to hit the light and said he could throw the ball anyplace except the lights. (This is the first time he has come anywhere near to testing the limits.)

He held the rubber elephant up to the easel and drew around it with a crayon. Then he started to draw around the alligator puppet, doing the head, added three long legs hanging down (which are not on the puppet), then quickly withdrew. He picked up the elephant again and drew in a little squiggle toward the rear of the picture. To do this he had to reach in between the

Very phallic drawings

Figure 1.

elephant's two rear legs. He said this was his tail (see Figure 1).

T commented that he was adding something at the rear end. He quickly dropped the whole project, but T kept on talking about his also not being able to finish the alligator with all his legs and bumps hanging down. This was all too much for Don to tolerate and he became very uneasy.

Play disruption

He went to the sand and acted out a scene with darts set up for traffic signs. The motorcycle cop knocked them all over without being aware of what he was doing, and so did all the things the signs were prohibiting.
A new little dart gun was on the shelf today but he couldn't find the darts for it. He finally gave up with an "Oh, well."

One must be more vigilant to control the unconscious

T said, "It must make you mad; let's face it; be mad." His response was to slap his own face(!). T again urged him to show his anger. Instead he phoned the police to report, "Somebody took the darts."

Can't admit to anger directly

He set up the dollhouse furniture on the table, adding all the little dolls as he counted the seven of them. He threw each doll back into the dollhouse, throwing father onto the bed. Mother was the last one and he threw her onto the bed with father saying, "She goes to father."

Oedipal rivalry

There was a final scene in the sand with the *Rivalry with*
baby carriage trying to do all the things the big *father*
cars could do. Everyone was telling it to "Go
back to your bottle."Finally the car drivers (men)
were convinced, and asked the price. The carriage said $1, but they offered $1,000.

T kept reflecting in terms of the little child
wanting to do everything grown men could do.

Don had eaten several cookies casually
throughout the hour. On leaving he took a final
"One for the road," was very jolly, and said a
cheerful "Goodbye" as he left.

Session 20

Don seemed quiet and subdued at first (reaction to father coming last time?). He was still uneasy about really hitting Bobo hard. He was wearing a badge that said "Uncle" and brought in two little rat-finks. He played out a sequence where they tried to convince the bank that they were really wealthy. They had forgotten that they had hidden their money in the cupboard, and told the bank it was in their safe. They also had forgotten the combination to the safe, so they built another safe. Of course this safe was empty when they opened it.

Things are not really what they seem

Don played with the balloons the rest of the hour. He put the rat-finks in the baby bottle, and clamped two round balloons on either side under the screw cap. He balanced this very genital-looking bottle contraption on top of the easel and spent a long time trying to shoot at, and burst, the balloons. The whole thing fell under the easel, so he crawled under, out of sight of T, and kept at it until the balloons finally burst, using the darts and the pinpoint of the Uncle badge.

Castration anxiety

T observed that he had to get it at exactly the right place, explosions were coming, etc. He said the rat-finks were very uneasy and didn't realize this was all for their own good.

Rat-fink = self; therapy is for his good

He finally dumped the rat-finks out of the bottle. In passing Bobo he jabbed at Bobo's fanny with

Sexual gesture

a dart. Then he blew into some of the long, but
burst, balloons which would only inflate mini-   *Masturbatory*
mally, and showed T how they were no good   *fears and guilt*
now.

He seemed relieved when T said he seemed
worried whether they would still be good for
anything now.

Then he found a large cat balloon which he blew
up but he couldn't find any string to tie it off. He
looked for and tried all kinds of things that might
do instead. Finally he said, "Oh well, never   *Does admit*
mind—but I *do* mind."   *caring*

T compared this as progress from his inability
to admit being mad last time.

By now, T had told him several times that it
was past time to leave. (He had always kept very
close track of the time previously.) Today he   *Reluctant to*
kept right on with his activities, not looking at   *end the ses-*
the clock at all. Finally he prepared to leave,   *sion*
looked in his pockets to see if he had everything,
and took a cookie "for the road." He had not
picked up the rat-finks and T reminded him of
them. He said, "Oh my, and I thought I had
everything."

Session 21

Don used the cars for most of the session. There were several racing sequences, and scenes of cars hiding under the sand and eventually being discovered. In the most significant sequence, a man was dashing to the hospital, was going too fast, missing the right turns, running over wet concrete, and finally was stopped by the police. The man said he couldn't be arrested because he was a "human being." The police told him everybody was. The man had been told there was a change in his son, and assumed this meant he was getting worse, while actually the boy was improving. So the man was put in jail for only three months, which was lenient because the man had been worried about his son.

Obviously refers to father's being asked to come in to discuss progress two weeks ago; Don realizes he's doing better

T commented on how the man just couldn't believe his son was getting better, that he was always expecting the worst, and now he had to be punished because he was concerned about his son.

Session 22

Don started to use Bobo, saying he wished it
were real. When sand started to leak out, he
became uneasy and changed to other activities.
He spent one-half hour shooting darts, mention-   *Rivalry with*
ing his brother repeatedly.   *brother*

   T made several comments on his probable
   feelings toward his brother, that he is stronger,
   teases Don, and takes advantage of him.

A little later he shot down two plastic bears in   Almost *ag-*
succession, saying "one"—"two"—then sud-   *gresses*
denly turned and pointed the gun directly at T   *against T*
with a "three." He didn't actually shoot it.

   T observed that she guessed he might like to
   shoot her, that maybe he was mad at her
   because she talked too much; that lots of boys
   feel that way about grown-ups. Don made no
   comments, but neither did he resort to his
   usual denials.

   He had brought a little yellow plastic gorilla
   which he called "King Kong" and played with
   this in the sand, and compared its size to the
   elephant and the dog. He seated it on a "throne"
   and poured sand over it, saying this was the
   food.

T pointed out the king had wanted food to be given freely but was now getting more than he had bargained for.

Then the "subjects" brought in a lot of furniture to please the king, but he wasn't satisfied and wanted a simpler arrangement. The king said it was his cousin that wanted things fancy.

King-father is never satisfied

He went back to the darts for the last few minutes, exclaiming, "I feel wild!" and was shooting recklessly, for him. He even aimed at the wall clock, saying, "How about shooting that?" but he didn't. He went to the cupboard to find more things to shoot, but was distracted by a new package of balloons with a squawker. When it was time to go he hid the squawking balloon in the doctor's kit, although he said he knew someone else might find it during the week. He seemed very relaxed and cheerful as he left.

Enjoys "letting go"

Session 23

Don brought in a very small water pistol (which
he didn't use) and a whistle, very much like the
squawker from the balloon of last time. He put
an inflated balloon on the whistle and looked
aghast when it made a very loud noise.

> He looked relieved when T said it was OK to
> make all the noise he wanted. He said he was
> just surprised.

He did blow up the whistle balloon several more
times and shot at the balloon with the dart gun.
  Next he started shooting darts at the target and
soon set up his own targets—a baby bottle and
three animals—on the table.

> T asked if his little brother still uses the bottle.
> C: No. T: Had he wanted to use one again
> when his brother was a baby? He denied this.

Much later in the hour he set the bottle on the
light switch and was shooting it off.

> T interpreted this in terms of his no longer
> doing babyish things, and his getting rid of all
> the babyness. This hit the mark and he pro-
> ceeded to boast about how good he feels when
> he is successful in target shooting with his
> brother and father. But even then he also had
> to mention that he had "failed" in a BB
> competition when he was seven, that he is still

*Expresses
pleasure at
being able to
compete, but
can't forget
his inadequa-
cies*

afraid to swim in deep water, and that he chose target shooting for a summer sport.

There was much vigorous swinging of Bobo. Once he came quite close to T with it and, addressing Bobo, "Don't you hide."

T: He can't run to mama for safety.

Once he said Bobo was bleeding.

T asked about his own nosebleeds now. He said he didn't have as many and wasn't as scared of them, except for hoping they wouldn't be long ones.

He said his brother would swing him across his shoulder as he was now doing to Bobo, and he did it once to his brother. Again said he wished Bobo were real.

More rivalry with brother

T: You'd show him how mad you are, and what you'd like to do to him.

He went back to the darts and to hitting the bottle off the light switch very accurately. He said he couldn't wait to tell his mother. T asked if his father wouldn't be pleased too. He hedged about this but a little later repeated the same comment under his breath but naming both parents.

Confides in mother more than father

When he was warned that it was time to leave, he said he had to do one more thing.

T commented that lately he seemed to hate to leave. He agreed to this.

Reluctant to leave

He took one more shot with the dart, went back for a cookie and left.

Session 24

Don began at once to shoot darts at the baby bottle.

    T talked more this time about his wanting to get rid of baby things; did people call him a baby or a sissy if he couldn't do things as well as others? C: Yes, but I show them I can.

Wants to put baby-stuff behind him

Pretty soon after that, he put four darts in his hand and told T that if he didn't hit the bottle with one of them, she would have to call him "chicken." He missed the first three shots; T said she didn't want to have to call him "chicken." He did miss the fourth shot and T did call him "chicken."

Maneuvers to get T to disparage him

    T also pointed out how he had seemed to get so excited and try so hard that he really couldn't do as well as he usually does. He admitted this, and got the bottle on the next try.

After a little more dart play, he saw a small medicine bottle. He put in some water and soap, calling this his Dr. Jekyll juice. He then added red paint which he called "blood," and some sand, and shook the bottle hard. He was quite concerned that some of the red paint would get on the other dishes but T reassured him it was all right. He offered this mix as a "delicious brew" to an "invisible friend" whom he dramatically seated at the table, after first opening the playroom door to admit the friend to the room. (NOTE: At this point T assumed the friend was

Blood play: starts out cautiously, offers blood as a trick in guise of food

Figure 2.

a boy.) The friend was suspicious and refused to drink. T and Don discussed this in terms of its poisonous aspects, and Don kept trying to reassure the friend that the brew was harmless.

Paraniod position; suspects food is bad, poisonous

T reflected on how words often sound good, but they may hide bad thoughts and schemes.

Finally Don wanted to get rid of the juice and asked where he could pour it; T suggested either the sink or toilet. He used the latter, and called the toilet an "alligator" as he flushed it, because it got rid of the stuff in one big gulp. At this point he acted as if the invisible friend had left the room. He checked the door, window, behind the cupboard, and door again to see where he might sneak back in.

Alligator = oral aggression

T: "You wonder if he can hear us from behind the door," and assured him nobody could hear; this was his room and hour.

More suspicions

He went to the easel and said he was going to paint a "blood picture." He kept swiping the red brush back and forth over the paper, making smears with some darker blobs in the middle (see Figure 2).

Very bloody! (Pure C à la Rorschach)

T: It looks real red on the sheet; is that the way the blood looks on your bed sheet when you get nosebleeds?

Figure 3.

He agreed to this and kept swishing the brush vigorously. Then he pointed out a shape that looked something like a face in the center, then to an inverted U-shape form in one corner, and mumbled that he didn't know what that was.

Bloodiness of nosebleeds blends with blood of urethral probes. Does he fear that sex is also bloody?

T said it looked like a penis.

Then he hurriedly turned the sheet back over the easel and started another picture. He said this was going to be a picture of his invisible friend (see Figure 3). This picture was also all red. He outlined the hair first and said, "I've got a secret—it's a *she*." He added eyebrows, only one eye, and a huge mouth.

Secret friend = mother

T said she looked sort of witchy; he countered with "She's a hag." He also indicated he liked her very much; she was his lady friend. T pointed out his ambivalence; he liked her so much yet he was also afraid of her, to which he agreed.

Bad mother versus good mother

Then he outlined a circular body and filled it in with solid red saying "This is all blood," using a tremendous amount of paint.

All the while T was saying that she was just full of blood; at different times it comes out of her; it's scary to see so much blood. He filled in the eye and added some teeth, as T kept commenting at great length on her being full of blood; it comes out of her nose at one end; and sometimes pours out of the other end; it gets all over everything.

Goes from own nosebleeds to mother's miscarriages and hemorrhages

Figure 4.

Then he added two legs and two arms at each side, saying now she looked like a spider.

Spider = bad mother

T emphasized he really seemed to like her in spite of her bloodiness and meanness.

The next painting done all in red (see Figure 4), was an outline of a house, his and his lady friend's, in a swamp. A large trapezoidal form near the bottom was the porch roof. A square window in the upper right was "her" room, the window at the left was his, and the center window between them was the living room.

Oedipal mother is inaccessible, forbidden

T pointed out that he would need to go through the living room to get to her.

He said that the whole thing looked like a face. He took time out to eat a cookie, "a poisoned one": his girl friend only let him have just one.

Orally depriving (and poisoning) mother

Then he said that he was going to paint a "monster"; that he "creates" these things. He started out with a purple crayon and the drawing soon became the face of a "butler" (see Figure 5). As he drew the eyes he said the butler couldn't see; his eyes were "stuck shut and sort of ruffly"; he was blind. He drew two big scars on the face, then a huge mouth with sharp teeth, top and bottom.

Shades of Oedipus!

T said it looked like he could really cut off things with those teeth; and since he was blind, he couldn't see his (Don's) lady friend.

Castration fears

Figure 5.

He used the red paintbrush to outline the mouth in red and added a line under one eye. There was more discussion of how the butler couldn't see the lady friend, how she could see Don, but Don wouldn't let the butler see her. Don said she liked the butler.

Butler = fused image of self and father Doesn't want father to "see" mother and wishes he himself could

T said that must make him feel very jealous and mad, and that he might try to keep her from the butler. After a good deal of this, he got quite dramatic and said, "I'll tell you a secret I've never told anyone before. He's her boyfriend!"

T observed he must be awfully jealous about that; he said, "But I'm *his* father." T said she guessed he would like to be able to boss the butler and control him, so he wouldn't get too close to her (i.e., the lady friend).

Admits the oedipal dilemma

Finally, he attacked Bobo, who was the butler, throwing him over his shoulder and around the room. Then he switched roles, saying, "This is what the butler does to me" (so Bobo became Don and the real Don became the butler). This Bobo play was started when he realized the time was almost up.

Fusion and reversals of father–son roles

Session 25

On the way to the playroom Don said it didn't seem like a whole week since last time; it seemed more like yesterday.

Feels comfortable here and anxious to come

T commented on how he had had a good session last time, and was able to get a lot of things out.

He spent most of the hour with play money and the cash register. T asked what he would do with all that money if it were real. He said he'd put all of his friends in jail. When T said that didn't make much sense, he was not able to give a good reason.

He directed T to call him on the toy phone and ask to buy a cookie. On the first call he actually gave her one (the first time he has offered any to her). Then he started raising the price each time, up to 50¢ each, and only pretending to give them to T when she gave him the money.

Gives T her first cookie, then makes impossible demands—as mother does to him?

T reflected in terms of his being stingy with food, and setting the price too high, as if he didn't really want her to have any; maybe people also do that to him, and don't give him all he wants.

He quickly dropped the cookie play and directed T to call her grandma; he took the part of the grandma. T asked if she could go see her, but "she" didn't want anyone to visit because she was sick.

Play disruption

T commented on grandma's meanness, and her not wanting to see her own family.

Grandparents (parents) are mean and unfriendly

This was all essentially repeated with T being directed to call her grandfather, and his also not wanting to see visitors. Then Don instructed T to call her cousin, and he used baby talk in playing the part of the cousin. The cousin said his mother wouldn't give him any bubblegum—not even one piece.

Mother with-holds food and treats

T talked about the mother being stingy.

Then he said T better call later as he (the cousin) was afraid his mother might hear them. T reassured him that they had a private line. He then said the mother didn't give him the gum because he had hit her with a baseball bat, and if she still wouldn't give him any gum he would do it again, or "scream my head off."

Concerned about confi-dentiality (as in last hour)

Wants to retaliate

As the hour was drawing to a close, he said it had gone too fast. With time for only one more call, T was directed to call *her* son. He answered as the son and said bank robbers had kidnapped him. T was concerned and asked where he was so she could come save him. He said it was a place with water all around. He was more afraid of the fish than of the kidnappers; in fact, a fish was eating him right then. T emphasized that she would be right over to help.

Cry for help! Would he like to be T's son and so "escape" from his parents?

At this, he got up, took a cookie, and ate it as he was leaving.

Session 26

While Don was tossing a ball, T asked how things were going, and how was school? He said everything at school was very, very, very, very good (about ten very's!). When pressed to be more specific, he was pretty vague, and couldn't state what subjects he liked best. He felt he was doing best in sounding out words, and this made spelling and reading easy.

Very positive feeling toward school

Then he got out the two phones, as in the last session, and directed T to call the police to report that her car was stolen. He, as the policeman, asked what kind of car she had. When she said a red Falcon he said that was the only kind of car they could not look for. The next call was to report that her house was on fire; again he refused help as all fifty fire trucks were out on call. Next, T was to call her cousin in Nebraska, pretending she was in New York; as the phone operator, he refused to put through her call until $300 was paid.

T used "red" deliberately
Does he hate to admit therapy has helped and so resists "helping" T?

In each of the above sequences, T called attention to his resisting, obstructing, and not wanting to be of help. (NOTE: This is the most obvious instance of resistance encountered so far, and he can only do this through the mediation of imaginary characters.)

Then Don called up T who was to be the grocer. He placed huge orders for all kinds of food, which T accepted and promised to fill, because she didn't want anyone to go hungry. He said it was all for one cow, and that he was a farmer.

Now permits T to help him as he demands oral supplies

Then Don called T as the doctor, because his dog had been bitten on the leg. Again, T tried to be helpful. He asked if she were a veterinarian, because this was a dog family calling.

Questions whether T is the right kind of doctor

Dropping the phone play he went to the easel, said he was an architect and T was to tell him what kind of house she wanted him to design. The first plans he drew were small and constricted; the next he made larger and more expansive at T's suggestion. When finished he quoted an exorbitant price.

T again reflected on his setting up impossible conditions and so offering resistance.

He inspected Bobo to see if it were fixed, so that "it won't bleed." He knocked it around a bit, especially poking it in the nose. Then some desultory play in the sand which someone else had wet down; he seemed not to like the feel of it and soon gave up.

Tests whether nosebleeds are cured

He used the water pistol and shot all around the room, at Bobo, the walls and shelves, and the easel.
T compared this to his earlier concerns about getting things wet with the pistol; that now he seemed to feel freer to shoot and let go.

Much freer in water play, even threatens to hit T

He kept on shooting, swinging around as he did so, and almost hit T as the gun swung in her direction. He commented on this.

T said she guessed he would really like to hit grown-ups sometimes.

Don had been eating single cookies several times during the hour. When it was time to go there were three cookies left. He went over to the dish and said, "I bet you can't guess how many I'm going to take with me this time." He took two in one hand then reached for the other one with the other hand.

Feels free to take all the cookies

T commented that he really did feel much freer now to do the things he wants to do.

Session 27

In dart play Don slipped the pistol up his sleeve
so that it was pointing toward himself.

T commented it looked like he wanted to hurt *Self-*
himself; did he ever get so mad he wanted to *destructive*
do that? He said only when he mislaid some- *gesture*
thing and couldn't find it.

He fixed a brew which he called "tomato *Feminine*
juice" from water, soap, and sand. After looking *play?*
over the paint jars and deciding not to add any
paint, he did finally pour in some red paint. He
said he was the cook, "Barbara." Then he got a *"Blood," as*
play cup and started to pour out some for T. In *food, leads to*
the process he spilled a couple of blobs on the *panic and*
floor, which brought on a real panic. He dashed *play disrup-*
around, hurried to get paper towels to wipe up *tion*
the floor, and quickly emptied the rest of the
goop in the toilet, going "Ugh" as he flushed it. *Bloody,*
menstrual
appearance

All this time T kept talking about his panic and
distress. He said that if he spilled paint on the
floor at home he would then bite his lip to
make it bleed and say that was the cause of the
redness. T talked about the self-hurting, and *Again, self-*
tied it in to the earlier discussion with the gun *injury to avoid*
pointed at himself. She also suggested that by *punish-*
hurting himself he gets sympathy and avoids *ment*
scoldings. She pointed out that his panic was
more than called for by the very little bit of
paint spilled; had he maybe sometime seen

blood on the floor at home and wondered
where it came from? He mumbled something
about getting blood on his hands, but not on
the floor, with his nosebleeds.

*Denies any
memories
of blood
(mother's
hemorrhages)*

There was some play with the doctor kit. He
was a doctor who couldn't see unless he wore
both pairs of glasses. He got confused and gave
shots to himself and tapped his own knee for
jerks, although T was the patient. He finally
asked T what "species" she was, and said he was
a veterinarian and not a doctor for humans.

T talked about there being different kinds of
doctors and you have to be sure to go to the
right kind. Maybe he was wondering what
kind of doctors we have here since they don't
give shots.

*Still
concerned
about kind of
doctors here.
Is he having
to explain his
clinic trips to
his school-
mates?*

He said he had two pictures at home of a doctor
with arms out (he extended his to illustrate) as if
he were shooting himself. He planned to bring
one and give it to T.
There was some final play with the fire en-
gines, with one of the firemen always in danger,
hanging onto the ladder as it swung around, etc.,
while the others tried to be of help.

Session 28

NOTE: This is the first time that Don has come in without being immaculately dressed. He has on dirty, patched jeans and a thin slipover sweater; he usually wears pressed pants, a collared shirt, and often tie and jacket. Father came in today to have a joint interview with mother's therapist.

Not as tidily dressed (any relation to Father coming in today?)

T mentioned that father was also coming today, and how did he feel about it? She also explained that they would be talking over how things were going now. How did he think things were going? He just said, "OK." Then T pressed him to be more specific: Did he get along better with kids now? Could he stand up for himself better? To the latter he said: "It's *too* much now." When asked about school he said things were much better, especially if he can sit off by himself to get his work done. Some of his friends laugh and joke too much when he's trying to study.

Reports improvements

He played quite a bit with a superball he had brought from home, then with the new balloons. He put two inflated ones in the screw top of the baby bottle and threw it up as a missile. He really didn't get involved in any major play sequences today.

No real involvement today

He did produce the doctor picture he had talked about last time and gave it to T as promised. It was a horrible monster in a white coat, brandishing a syringe in each hand, with a

Quite a gift for T!

stethoscope in his ears, huge eyes, and a mouth with a big, red, pointed tongue sticking out between lots of sharp teeth. He said he sometimes dreams of doctors looking like that and giving shots. He shuts his eyes when he's getting a shot.

T said that was one way of handling things, but then you'll never really know for sure what went on. T also said she guessed he was still wondering what kind of doctors we have here since they don't give shots and just talk. He said he guessed T was "half and half"; T explained that she was a psychologist. When she asked if the kids ever asked him why he came here or what kind of doctor he was going to, he mumbled an affirmative.

Admits to peers' curiosity about his clinic trips

As for the cards, evidently there is a series, and he said he tries to find appropriate ones for his acquaintances. He gave a granny one to his grandmother and found ones with the correct names on them for two of his cousins. Then he showed T about a dollar-and-a-half in change, which he had in his pocket, from his allowance.

Session 29

NOTE: Two sessions were missed over spring vacation.

Don did not have much to say about the vacation, but he did volunteer that he celebrated his birthday recently. His main comments were about the toys he received that didn't work, such as a gun which he only got to use once before his brother dropped it and broke it so that it cannot be repaired. Another toy was defective so they had to return it, but his mother let him choose whatever he wanted at the same price.

Things go wrong even on his birth-day

Through all of this, T tried to elicit his reactions and possible feelings of anger or frustration, but he showed very little affect.

Then he tried to shoot at inflated balloons, but missed and said, "Failed again."

Resignation

After several such instances of no success, T summarized how everything seemed to always go wrong for him. He commented, "That's the way the ball bounces." T still kept pushing for feelings, and later, when he was succeeding, called attention to the difference in the way he felt and acted now.

Rationalizes, but philosoph- ically now

He engaged in phone sequences in which he would direct T as to whom she was to be and in general what she was to say:

1. A mother asking another mother to let her boy come to a birthday party.

Arranges to be in control of T by restricting and depriving

2. Calling the phone company for an extension phone, but the company didn't have the colors she wanted and the price was exorbitant.

3. Calling a pet shop for a huge animal; again the price he quoted was too high.

In each instance his response involved setting prices out of reason, or choices were not available, or T would have to wait a very long time for her order. T summarized these aspects. In subsequent sequences, the situations become more realistic, items were available and reasonably priced.

Moves to more realistic balance

Session 30

NOTE: It has been three weeks since the last
session.

Don spontaneously commented that it seemed a
long time since he had last been here. Last week
he couldn't come because he had fallen off his
bike a few days before and was quite bruised up;
he still has sores on his arms. He went on to
explain that the accident happened just three
hours after he had passed his bike safety test. His
father had remarked, "Some safety!" He didn't   *Can report*
seem to have minded similar comments and   *father's sar-*
teasing from his classmates. To T's inquiry, he   *casm*
denied that there had been much blood, or that
this had bothered him.

He spent most of the session with the sand. He
found the silvery metal bottom sheet from a toy
phone and set it up as the "iron curtain" to keep
jeeps from getting supplies in to the people
behind the curtain. Soon the sheet became a
broad diving board, which he anchored securely
on both sides with sand.

It was now the middle of May and school
would soon be over. With a view to exploring
possible termination, T asked how things were
going now at home and at school. He said his
teacher had called his mother after spring vaca-
tion to report how well he was doing, and that   *Animated re-*
"made my mother very, very, very, very, very   *port of*
happy and that makes me very, very, very, very,   *progress*

very happy." He said this in a happy, light-
hearted tone, with ten or fifteen "verys" in each
instance.

T asked if it didn't make his father happy, too;
he agreed but in a very noncommittal fashion.
T suggested that maybe he didn't need to keep
coming here if things were going so well at
school, and with the other kids, and at home.
Also, he didn't seem to be so afraid of blood   *Still some*
anymore. To this last, he denied ever being   *denial; he's*
really afraid; then: "Well, anybody wouldn't   *human too*
want to get hurt."

As for terminating, he said he would have to   *Termination*
see what his mother thought. T said it was really   *discussion*
up to him to decide if he needed to come, and his
mother could decide how long she needed to
keep coming for her therapy. It was left that he
would come in the next week, omit the following
week which would be Memorial Day, then come
the next week. By that time he would have had
time to think about it, talk it over with his
mother, and make a decision as to what to do for
the rest of the summer, or if he needed to come
anymore at all.

Session 31

Don's mother did not come in today, so he was sitting alone in the waiting room; T was about five minutes late in picking him up. He expressed real concern, saying, "You're always earlier," and went on to say he had wondered if she were really coming.

Can express his uneasiness (probably afraid T had already terminated)

Once in the room he started hitting Bobo quite hard.

T said she guessed he was really mad at her for being late.

Projects anger onto Bobo

He kept on hitting quite hard, but gradually changed into a demonstration of different karate punches. Then he got a handful of darts and shot all twelve, hitting the target each time. He was quite happy and pleased with himself.

Can show self-satisfaction

He looked for the "iron curtain" and used it as a pizza pan, measuring and counting out spoonfuls of sand quite compulsively, pouring these on the pizza. He said this was for the General, and only the crumbs were for the dog. When T expressed sympathy for the dog he became more generous. Then he measured water and sand into the baby bottle for an "experiment." He finally went into the bathroom and closed the door while he worked on a "secret formula." When he came out he said it hadn't worked, "You can't win all the time."

Denies oral gratification to "underdog" (self?)

Ready to try "new" things and philosophical about failure

T commented on his feeling so free and willing to try new things, and not getting too upset if they weren't perfect.

He put a long, red balloon in the baby bottle and blew it up so that it expanded up beyond the lip of the bottle into a quite long, red, phallic-looking appendage. He kept squeezing this to watch it retract and expand. He said, "It's enough to last the baby all night."

Earlier "secret" leads to masturbatory symbolism

T kept remarking on its getting long and hard, then it goes limp when you squeeze it.

Finally the balloon deflated completely and fell into the bottle. He dug it out with his fingers; it was damp and he gingerly dropped it into the wastebasket.

T said it looked like he didn't like the feel of it after it got wet.

Then he inflated a balloon which he stuck through the toy eyeglasses, holding them up to his face and saying it didn't look like him.

T asked if he had thought anymore about whether he still needed to come. He said he didn't think he needed to; he was doing his schoolwork real well; and he had "self-confidence" now. (He stumbled over the pronunciation of this and laughed about it.) T asked if he just wanted to come in the one more time after Memorial Day, but he hesitated and delayed answering. T asked if he was feeling that this was his last time, and he said that was it. T

Offers good reasons for terminating

T is reluctant to accept his earlier timing

agreed that this was all right and assured him she would be available to see him if he ever felt the need to come back.

When the hour was up he said, "I want to make one last cake." He poured sand in a smooth layer on the pizza pan then took a stick and wrote "Goodbye." He smiled up at T and was ready to leave.

Arranges his own farewell, and on an oral basis!

Session 32

Follow up, two months later.

NOTE: Due to a mix-up in communications, Don had accompanied his mother to the clinic the week following Memorial Day. He was told that his therapist had understood that he would not be coming, but that she could probably be reached if he wanted to see her. Her decided not to have her called.

Don was cheerful and happy and full of talk about his summer's activities. He told of his brother's birthday and that he also got some presents from someone who had overlooked him on his own day.

T asked about the day he came last spring, after she thought they had planned to terminate; she wondered if she had misunderstood what he intended at that time. He indicated it was his mother who was unsure and she had suggested that he go with her the next week to make certain. He reacted positively to the discussion of this incident. T also expressed regret that she thus had not been able to see the clipping he had brought in on that day. He went into a long description of the events leading up to the bicycle rodeo; his coming in second and having his picture in the paper. He was quite pleased with his performance in the races, and could report it with justifiable pride. He then launched into a discussion of his developing prowess in

Now ready to be "one of the boys"

swimming and shooting, and that he would like
to try wrestling next.

He spent the hour looking at all the play   *Good food*
equipment. He finally settled on the sand and   *and bad food*
spent the time measuring it into different dishes
as food and then as a witch's potion.

T asked if he felt that he would need to come
in regularly this next school year. He didn't feel
he did, and T agreed. He is looking forward to
school. In fact he thinks it would be better if
there were no long vacations, then kids wouldn't
be griping about having to go back again. He   *Accepts life*
said the first day usually isn't very good, but you *philosophi-*
soon get used to things again.   *cally*

NOTE: It was interesting that, although he tried
out nearly every piece of equipment he had used
previously, he made no attempt to eat the cookies, nor did he mention them.

Final Therapy Report

Don was seen for a total of thirty-two sessions, on a weekly basis. He was eight years, nine months of age when therapy was begun and was repeating second grade. Referral problems included poor schoolwork in spite of better-than-average intellectual ability, feelings of inadequacy, and many fears of blood, pain, and bodily injury. He was reported to have frequent nosebleeds and to have been very concerned over his mother's several miscarriages, at which times he had seen much blood.

In the early sessions, Don was very precise, constricted, and compulsively neat (wiping up small bits of sand, replacing all toys on the shelves before leaving, etc.). He displayed very little affect, could not express any anger, or admit to any disappointments. He would persistently deny any feelings or ascribe them only to others. By the conclusion of therapy he was dressing less neatly, leaving messes of sand and paint in the room, and freely shooting water at walls and toys. He became much more able to face, admit, and discuss his feelings, both pleasant and unpleasant (e.g., in the 20th session he was unable to find the materials he needed for a project and finally said, "Oh well, never mind . . . but I *do* mind"; or when shooting darts recklessly [for him], "I feel wild").

He dramatized many play sequences using small people, cars, and animals, accompanying the activities with considerable verbal description and spontaneous fantasy. The main play themes included animals and people changing form and species (identity problems); father figures portrayed as generals, masters, and presidents (oedipal rivalries); food deprivations (from bad-mother figures); adults never satisfied with the performance of underlings, with the latter retaliating in kind; and self-defeating maneuvers. These themes were repeated over and over again until he finally worked through his feelings of being a weakling and a sissy, and then began dramatizing acceptance by peers, and the ability to stand up to his older brother and even surpass him at times.

It is worth noting that Don never really engaged in activities designed to test limits. Even very tentative attempts were not employed until the 19th session when he acted as if he might shoot at the lights or (Session 22) in the direction of the therapist for the first time. The only instances of resistance occurred symbolically in his play through the medium of pretend characters who tried to obstruct the therapist's wishes during phone conversations.

Much of the play symbolism suggested strong guilt feelings and the need for punishment, masturbatory impulses, and castration fears. Repeated efforts were made to encourage him to discuss his fears of blood; at first he would deny all feelings or would discuss the fears of others in similar circumstances. Finally, in the 24th session, his reactions to blood, his attraction to his mother, and his jealousy of his father were all elicited in a dramatic session which started with his mixing up a concoction which he called "blood" and offered as a "delicious brew" to an "invisible friend." This was followed by a series of four rapidly painted pictures: (1) blood; (2) the invisible friend with a body full of blood, a female toward whom he expressed strongly ambivalent feelings; (3) the house he and she occupied but in which she was relatively inaccessible; (4) a "blind butler" who was his "lady friend's boyfriend" but also Don's son. In an ensuing encounter between Don and this butler, the roles of father and son became quite fluid and interchangeable with unmistakable oedipal overtones.

There was a distinct change in the remaining sessions, as if the major problems had now been faced and worked through. In a few weeks he was spontaneously reporting that things were going very well at school. He was obviously feeling more competent and self-assured. During the 30th session the therapist discussed his possible feelings about termination, which he also seemed to feel ready for but wanted to discuss first with his mother. The therapist suggested he do this and plan on coming at least two more times before reaching a final decision. Toward the end of the next session he indicated that he had planned that this would be his last one, because he now had so much "self-confidence," and he wrote out "Goodbye" in the sand before he left. The therapist, then, also structured this as his last session. Nevertheless, the following week, he accompanied his mother when she came in for her session and acted as if he had expected to see his therapist. He had brought a clipping from the paper about himself to show her. It was explained that she was not expecting him but that she could be reached if he wanted to see her. He decided not to have her called.

A follow-up session was scheduled after the summer break. He was eager to talk about his summer activities and accomplishments; did not seem upset by the mix-up in the spring appointment, saying it was his mother who thought he should come in. He didn't see any need to continue therapy in the fall.

Notes From Mother's Therapist

The psychiatrist who was seeing Don's mother has kindly offered these observations from his weekly sessions with her:

The mother, an exceptionally attractive and charming thirty-one-year-old, admitted being quite disappointed when she realized she was pregnant with Don—conceived when his older brother was only two months old. Throughout the first two trimesters she was frequently in solitary tears, appalled at the idea of having a second child so close to her first. Her distress was in marked contrast to the reception her first pregnancy had received.

She was a college graduate, married on her schedule to the right man who provided well for her. The eagerly anticipated first pregnancy was part of her plan, her second pregnancy was not. During her late seventh month, while picnicking in the park, she hemorrhaged all over a friend's blanket and tablecloth. Diagnosed placenta previa, she was placed in the hospital labor room; TV and radio were removed. No visitors were allowed except fifteen-minute perfunctory daily visits from her husband. She recalled the obstetrician ambivalently reassuring her with, "We think we can save you, but we aren't sure about the baby."

"God, why is this happening to me?" she recalled. "My rejection of the baby. Divine punishment."

"A bargain, God. Let my baby live and I'll be the best mother ever."

But for certain, Don's older brother was given greater freedom, often accompanying his father to his several service stations, while Don remained reined in close to his oath-bound mother.

Her husband was a relatively minor issue. He filled the role of a provider, a resource to his wife, and a father to his eldest son. However, the mother stood between him and the second son, frequently not only protecting him from inappropriate discipline, but more often from appropriate father–son interaction. It took at least six months of therapy to peel her off of Don, and for her to allow him to go with his older brother and his father on their many outings, both to the service stations and to the drag racing.

Fortunately, she gradually was able to begin focusing a little better on her two-year-old toddler and enjoying her motherhood which, in spite of her many traumatic pregnancies before conceiving this third child, appeared to be a fairly healthy balance of support and resource and modest limit setting.

Chapter 3

Individual Themes

Introduction and Overview

Various themes related to ego functioning and psychosexual development can be traced throughout the sessions. Some of the themes document progress with respect to specific referral problems; others arose after a certain amount of release from hitherto repressive defenses.

In the course of therapy, these various themes evolve and become intertwined like strands that have been overlapped and interlaced to form a "therapeutic braid." The following attempt to trace these threads is a process similar to undoing the braid and looking at each separate strand, while at the same time not overlooking the points at which the strands have crossed and recrossed.

Don's main presenting problems were his poor self-image, withdrawal from peers, and deteriorating performance in school. The first theme—Self-Concept—follows the path of progress in these areas. His Compulsive Cleanliness, and the underlying Urethral–Anal components, serve as the focus of the second theme. The resolution of these two themes might be seen by some therapists as the end goal of therapy, but other strands from deeper layers of personality were added to the braid as therapy proceeded.

Throughout the sessions the therapist was constantly on the alert for any clues from his play that might be related to his phobic fear of blood and, using knowledge from his history, watching for opportunities to reinforce, or inject, references to the past traumas in this area. In this connection, it was also expected that fears and anxieties related to castration might be uncovered; hence the title of the third theme—Reactions to Blood and Castration Fears.

By the climatic session (24), the theme of blood had become thoroughly melded and incorporated into the next two strands to be discussed: Oedipal issues centering on the good- and bad-mother figures; and Rivalry and attempts at Identification with his very masculine father. Indications of Masturbatory Concerns were almost totally confined to the last "trimester" of therapy.

Finally, Oral aspects, including the progress demonstrated in his reactions to food and cookies, are discussed. This was a child who had suffered massive oral deprivation as an infant; nearly all sessions contain some orally relevant material— either related to oral aggression or wanting to be fed and satisfied. Tracing this particular strand serves in some fashion as a summary view of his progress throughout the sessions.

A deliberate attempt has been made to present each theme so that it can be read as a separate and complete entity to facilitate group discussions. However, a particularly significant session in one area often served as a catalyst to a more concentrated emphasis on yet another theme. Consequently, the necessary repetition of certain therapy events that are relevant to more than one theme may help in tying all the strands into one complete whole.

Overview of Therapy

The early sessions are largely devoted to helping Don recognize his fears, phobias of dirt, and feelings of inadequacy, while challenging his defenses (rationalizations, denials, and projection onto others). As he is encouraged to assert himself, the play symbolism becomes clearly set in terms of challenging father figures in feats of skill. When mother images appear it is in the context of orally depriving, witchy figures.

Don's improvement in self-esteem and self-confidence becomes apparent by the 12th to 17th sessions as he struggles to bury his "sissy" self. Emphasis on cookie eating—by proxy or directly—has lost most of its need-gratifying appeal by this time.

Only after working through the rivalries with father do new themes of castration fears and some masturbatory concerns make their appearance. Session 10, especially, seems to be the demarcating point between the power issues with and against father and the introduction of themes of blood and castration. This was dramatically demonstrated in the multidetermined symbolic play of jabbing knives in the groin area of a figure buried in the sand. This particular play episode encapsulates fears of castration, reliving of his infantile intrusive body trauma, and fears for mother's pregnancies and miscarriages (with possibly some feelings of guilty responsibility). Masturbatory themes peak from the 18th to 20th sessions and oedipal themes reach a climax in the 24th.

In summary, once his preoccupation with compulsive cleanliness is worked through and a degree of self-esteem achieved, he can then address the deeper levels of affects and impulses centered around the infancy traumas, oedipal conflicts, castration anxieties, and masturbatory fantasies. He continues to work through his conflicts around sissiness, practices the skills of strength that would enable him to take his place in a "man's world," then advances to a classical portrayal of the oedipal triangle as he and the father figure fight for mother's affection.

Theme I. Self-Concept

In the initial session, Don is constrained and restricted. His first, and only, toy choice is the dart gun. Subsequent early sessions are replete with self-defeating maneuvers, denials of affect, and rationalizations of his constricted behavior while parentally unapproved behavior is projected onto "other kids." One can never know the real price of things (Session 1); play figures eat the clock then they don't know what time it is (2); or eat the refrigerator so there's no place to keep food (2). Self-figures are seen as being deliberately dumb and stupid (3); the fruitless search for friends culminates in self-destruction (4); characters are never satisfied with their lot (4); and he seems to see himself as still being a cry-baby and a weakling when he grows up (5).

By Session 6 he can tentatively admit to enjoying getting his friend wet with a water gun. In the same session he verbalizes and exhibits his first genuine pleasure in his accomplishment with the darts ("This is fun"), and shows more and more pride and excitement as T cheers him on. He then sets up a final play situation where he would be unable to hit the father figure. This is the first session in which he has felt free enough to eat cookies directly, rather than by proxy, but only if he misses a shot!

In the next session (7), Don seems at ease in discussing a disappointing hunting trip during which his older brother was clearly favored, but he denies any anger and makes excuses for the adults' restrictions when T points out that he must have felt bad. In the following session (8) he brags about being able to draw better than his brother, but again offers denials and excuses when T contrasts these feelings with his previous expressions of feeling inadequate and left out. This time T speculates that, in spite of his reasons, she suspects he really does feel bad most of the time. While drawing Bobo, he admits he made a "booboo" when he used this spelling as the title for the figure.

When Don first attempts to use the water pistol (9), he draws back initially saying he could have as much fun with the dart gun, but T points out how he often makes excuses to hide what he really wants to do. Thus encouraged, he thoroughly enjoys the activity. His final play sequence pits good animals against bad as he works through conflicts over now being encouraged (or free) to do forbidden things.

By the 12th session his identity concerns clearly come to the fore (with some assist from T!). After several sequences in which figures fool other people or are not what they appear to be, T uses the symbolism as a means of confronting the core of his ineffectual feelings. She first observes that the people are trying to do impossible tasks, then that they are pretending to be somebody else. Next she relates this to girls and boys sometimes wishing to be the opposite sex, and finally points out that sometimes boys may be called "sissies" when they know they are really boys. (This may have been a quantum leap on T's part, but events of subsequent sessions confirmed her hunch.) Although he avoids looking at T, he does not make the usual denials; rather, he almost imperceptibly nods agreement. Don then initiates a sequence in which an Indian (self?) displays his strength and manliness against a ferocious horned dinosaur.

The next session (13) continues the "sissy" theme which has now been brought out into the open where it can be worked through, not just verbally but demonstrated physically as well. A robed priest–magician figure performs feats of strength while declaring he doesn't like to be called a *weakling, shorty, or ugly,* to which T adds *sissy.* Don readily includes this term as he has the magician repeat his acts of defiance until he is finally accepted by his peers; thus a feminine-appearing (robed) figure can really be strong and masculine. From this activity he shifts to his first *direct* punching of Bobo. (Previous use has consisted of drawing it, shooting it with darts, or hitting it via proxy figures.) The hitting becomes quite vigorous until finally, now using a plastic figure, he hits at Bobo saying, "Don't call me a sissy." (At the time, T felt this was a truly cathartic session; in retrospect, it was indeed a milestone in his journey toward mastery, autonomy, and masculine identity.)

These direct and vigorous physical attacks on Bobo are continued for the next two sessions (14 and 15), with the approaching end of each hour eliciting planned vicious final attacks. After the interruption of the Christmas holidays, the 16th session is largely devoted to a discussion of a crisis in the neighborhood. He at first denies he was afraid when the family reported a theft to the police, and projects his fear onto his little brother. With help from T he can finally admit to feeling funny, and then to feeling nervous, and he guesses that is a kind of fear. In a final play scene in this session (16), the witch (bad mother) attacks the horned devil and turns him into a little girl (sissy?) while the King and his more powerful Queen look on.

Don returns to Bobo full force in the next two sessions (17 and 18). Not only is Bobo attacked with fists, but wildly thrown against chairs, "cut up" and eaten, and finally buried in a coffin. His comment, as he pushes Bobo's face in, that "Your mother won't know you" confirms the hypothesis that he has been destroying his old sissy self, is aware that the changes he feels in himself will show, and that this may be more than mother bargained for. When he says he wishes Bobo were real, T carries this one step further to suggest he'd like to show his friend how strong he has become. He agrees but with qualifications: "Not so much he'd no longer be friends." In subsequent balloon play, he jabs at one with a knife and, for the first time, spontaneously expresses angry feelings: "Now I'm *really* mad." He leaves each of these sessions in a happy, light-hearted mood.

It is interesting that only with this direct catharsis via Bobo does he feel spontaneous enough to take cookies with him as he leaves, while joking unself-consciously, "One for the road." By this time in therapy he has moved from a shy and terribly constricted child who must deny all feelings and rationalize his shortcomings, to a boy who is proud of his skills, confident in manner, and free to express his feelings and desires. He has indeed figuratively buried his old self. But, as will be apparent, such gains are not without relapses, although the general thrust of his behavior has now been set in a forward direction.

By Session 19 Don becomes more daring and makes his first tentative attempts to "rebel" as he dares to test the limits by aiming the ball at the light, but not actually throwing it. In subsequent sessions he almost shoots a dart at T and at the wall clock (22), almost pushes Bobo against T (23), and narrowly misses T with the water pistol (26). By this time he feels free enough to comment on what he has done.

In Session 19 he reports school and Cub Scout accomplishments with pride and ends the session taunting the baby carriage to "Go back to your bottle" as it tries to complete with adult vehicles, but the "baby" ends up being accepted.

With his new found self-confidence in his abilities he also is able to openly admit and verbalize his feelings. In Session 19 he starts to give up when frustrated because he can't find the darts. T encourages him to show his anger with, "Let's face it, be mad." Instead he slaps his own face in a curious literal twist of meaning (!) and phones the police to report the theft. Yet in the next session (20), when again frustrated, he starts to rationalize then spontaneously shifts to verbalizing his feelings: "Oh well, never mind . . . but I *do* mind." At the end of Session 22 he is shooting darts all over the room and can express his feelings of abandon, "I feel wild!"

At about this time, and two weeks after father and mother had had a joint session with her therapist, Don plays out several racing car sequences (Session 21). In one of these a man is driving fast to get to the hospital because there has been a "change" in his son. The man assumes this means his son is getting worse, while actually the boy was improving. (Don is now realizing the change in himself.)

The concerns about being viewed as a baby or sissy reappear in only two subsequent sessions. In Session 23, as he sets up a baby bottle as a dart-gun target, T talks first about his little brother using a bottle, then about his no longer doing babyish things and wanting to get rid of all babyness. His immediate response is to boast about his recent successes in competing with his older brother and father and he also is planning to tell his mother of his prowess in the playroom. When he returns to shooting at the bottle early in the next session (24), T reemphasizes his now wanting to get rid of baby ways, and asks if he used to be called a baby or a sissy. He admits to this but says he now can show them that he's not.

It is probably no accident that events thus far in therapy have served to usher in, at this point in Session 24, the strikingly climactic episode of the "Blind Butler" (see theme of Reactions to Blood and Castration Fears).

Overall improvement in his attitudes and his gains in self-assurance become quite marked in the following sessions. On arriving for Session 25 he comments that the past week went quickly, and, during the hour, he notes that the time is going by too fast. He also initiates, in this session, a series of sequences in which he takes the lead in interactions with T, directing her as to what to do and say in phone conversations (25, 26, 29).

In answer to T's inquiry (Session 26), Don proudly states that he is now doing very well in school and elaborates further (Session 28) by volunteering that he can stand up for himself "almost too much now." Session 28 is also the first session in which he appears in dirty, patched clothes in contrast to his immaculate "well-dressed" appearances in all previous sessions.

His ability to accept failure is approached during Session 29 when he is unsuccessful in hitting balloons with the darts and comments, "Failed again." When T points out how things often seem to go wrong for him, he philosophically responds, "That's the way the ball bounces." T continues the discussion, pointing out his successful shots and how different he feels when things do go well. The concept of self-acceptance reappears in Session 30 when T is listing various indicators of his improvement and remarks, in the context of his recent bicycle accident, that he doesn't seem so afraid of blood now. He first counters with denials, then says, "Anybody wouldn't want to get hurt."

Since the school year is drawing to a close T inquires as to how things are going at school and at home (Session 30). Don proudly reports that his teacher had called his mother to tell her how well he was doing and that made both his mother and himself very, very (ad infinitum!) happy. This leads to a discussion of probable termination, which generates some dependency on his part (i.e., mother should be consulted). T tells him it is really up to him to decide, and they agree to at least two more sessions. He arrives at the following session (31) stating he doesn't feel he needs to come anymore because he now has "self-confidence."

Theme II. Compulsive Cleanliness and Anal–Urethral Aspects

Don's initial toy choice in Session 1 is the dart gun, which he handles in a stilted, self-conscious, and methodical manner. He shows surprise at seeing water pistols on the shelf and attempts to allay the enuretic anxiety aroused by projection to other children, ambivalence, and a compulsive discussion of the unpredictable prices of these toys in the stores. The same neat and compulsive reactions are apparent in the next session (2) in the selection of puppets and their return to their box after each sequence. Toward the end of the session he does demonstrate some impulses to "let go" and mess via the witch and the dollhouse furniture, with particular emphasis on the bathroom fixtures. He soon retreats and restores order to the rooms. When T discusses his ambivalence, he restates his position quite cogently: "I'm really messy, but I don't like to make messes," and appears to accept T's comments about the probable guilt feelings involved.

With the introduction of a tub of sand in Session 3, Don first expresses dislike, then adopts a patronizing tone toward the probably favorable reactions of other children. He finally distances himself still further by justifying his attitude as concern about the extra work for the janitors, thus allying himself with the disapproving adults. However, he does eventually drive cars and trucks through the sand. In subsequent contests between toy animals he rewards the winners with small pieces of cookie, which he then pops into his own mouth. He had ignored the cookies when they were initially introduced in the previous session. Finally, even the cookies are cast as being potentially messy when one of the "recipients" crumbles his share on the floor and hides the crumbs under the bed. In the last few minutes of the hour the apparent self-figure for the session buries himself in the sand (masked desire to be messy?) and volunteers that it doesn't feel too bad to be covered with "dirt."

Sessions 4 and 5 contain little, if any, references to cleanliness. The play revolves around competition with father figures and veiled references to mother's many pregnancies. In the context of an apparent self-figure (Wolf-man) he tries to no avail to win friends by sharing all the money in the world.

The introduction of a new water pistol in Session 6 initiates a discussion of an incident in which he accidentally (?) had gotten his friend wet, along with denials of any aggressive feelings being involved. (It will take three more sessions before he will feel free enough to actually use the water pistol himself.) On leaving this session he brushes floor dust off his knees and guiltily admits that his mother would scold if she thought he had deliberately tried to get dirty.

In the next session (7), considerable sand play with cops and firemen putting out fires ends with the play figures being covered with wet sand. Careful attention is paid to brushing the sand off the toys and finally washing them in the sink (reaction-formation and undoing). He denies any disgust with dirt and/or fear of scolding by retreating to excuses of concern for "other kids" not liking to find dirty toys in the playroom. In the following sessions (8), a skunk figure (messy and smelly) is initially rejected by the other animals, then acts sneaky and eats all the cookies, but is finally accepted.

The initial play in Session 9 involves cars and trucks attacking each other in the wet sand, and his being upset by their messiness. As he puts them away he only shakes the sand off rather than wiping them. When he starts to pick up the water pistol, then draws back while giving excuses, T encourages him and confronts him with his typical pattern of using excuses to cover his fear of admitting to what he would really like to do. He does return to the gun and water play, but propitiates his urethral concerns by first compulsively covering the table so that it won't get wet. He then shows real pleasure as he shoots the toy animals. He is careful to wipe up all the splattered water when he is through. In the next sequence he sets up good animals fighting bad ones (especially aiming for the bull), as he tries to work through his conflicts over wanting to do what parents (and conscience) have always forbidden.

Perhaps as a reaction to the previous session with its emphasis on letting go in the wetting and messing areas, Session 10 begins with a very organized and controlled animal farmyard where the pigs are isolated in their own separate mud hole. (At least they are permitted to be pigs in their own pig pen!) The sequence ends with further compulsive ordering of all the figures from the largest to the smallest. It is noteworthy that the remainder of this session is filled with the most aggressive and dramatic play so far observed (and highly suggestive of castration fantasies and/or the reliving of his infantile urethral traumas), as he jabs knives into the groin area of a "person" buried in the sand (see the theme of Reactions to Blood and Castration Fears).

At the close of Session 12 Don unself-consciously goes to the sink to wash sand off his hands; previously this has been under the pretext of cleaning up the toys. Symbolic themes around money, all with anal connotations, appear about this time in the context of a rich man attempting to cheat a poor man out of his money (12); and using toy money as a consolation to Bobo after "killing" him (15). In Session 16 he discusses his concerns about a neighbor boy stealing money and a minibike from the family. (He then needs to go to the bathroom for the first and only time during his sessions.) He expresses pride in his Christmas gifts largely in terms of their cost; and plays animatedly with the toy money, throwing it recklessly (for him) into the air.

By Session 17, he seems more tolerant of messes as he apparently enjoys the predicament of the skunk who is unable to get any animal to clean up his dirty house even if he pays them. Soon he has the dollhouse father also complaining that his house is dirty. In the next session (18), when Bobo is leaking sand, Don is not too upset either from the messy or the damage aspects.

Later episodes in this session revolve around his first use of long, phallic-shaped balloons which he fills with water and drops, not boldly on the floor as T suggests, but in the sink. He seems to genuinely enjoy this play, especially when the balloons burst.

After four sessions devoted largely to oedipal situations and phallic–masturbatory symbolism, he discovers some squawking balloons and appears shocked, yet intrigued, by the flatulent sound made when they deflate (Sessions 22 and 23).

In Sessions 25 and 26 (and again in Session 29), Don plays out several sequences of "withholding" behavior, in which he would set exorbitant prices for goods and services which he directs T to request on the toy phones, and pay for with toy money. Then different imaginary relatives are stingy and obstinate in refusing to see anyone. He is also much freer with the water pistol now, shooting at the walls, playshelves, and toys, as well as coming close to hitting T, an event that he handles with aplomb. There is no attempt on his part to wipe up any of the water. However, in Session 27, he panics when he spills a little of a mixture of red paint, soap, and sand on the floor. He scurries around to wipe up the spots and empties the jar in the toilet with vocal disgust. T uses this sequence, not in terms of his compulsive need to be clean (since he seems to have worked through major feelings in this area), but rather she relates his excessive reaction in this episode to his possibly having seen blood on the floor at home. He ignores these implications and continues to blame his concerns on his nosebleeds.

The next session (28) is noteworthy in that it marks the first time that Don has come to his sessions in dirty, patched clothes, and with no jacket or tie. He also proudly shows T the allowance money in his pocket.

In the final session (31), when one often sees a reprise of the early presenting problems, he does revert to compulsively measuring and counting scoops of sand for a pizza he is making for the General; only the crumbs would be given to the dog! He mixes sand and water for an experiment, then takes it into the adjoining bathroom to work on a "secret formula." T is never permitted to view this secret; he philosophically informs her that it hadn't worked out as he had hoped. Finally, he continues to make constructive use of this messiest of mediums as he scratches "Goodbye" on his "one last cake of sand."

Theme III. Reactions to Blood and Castration Anxiety

In view of Don's history of experiences with bodily insults, both to himself and to members of his family, his own nosebleeds, and his knowledge of his mother's miscarriages, the therapist was particularly alert to any play behavior with symbolic representations that she could take advantage of as possible openings for comments, observations, and explorations of the accompanying affects. (Psychoanalytic logic might suggest putting this section on castration fears along with masturbatory fantasies in conjunction with discussions of rivalry with the father. In this particular case, the preoccupation with blood is far more multidetermined and seems to underlie all of Don's oedipal concerns.)

In Session 1 the initial choice of dart gun and darts may be related to his infantile experience with the urethral probe; but this is highly speculative since all little boys seem to be attracted to this activity. Nevertheless, this rather typical play choice is highly structured by this child, as if he were defending against any display of pleasure or enjoyment. In the next session (2), the focus of the play, in addition to use of the witch-mother, is on the alligator with a bright red mouth. This figure is fed a hot, peppery brew that stings his mouth, suggestive of the unpleasant sensations connected with the recent tonsillectomy, or quite possibly with the infantile probes (albeit with displacement from genital to oral areas). T only comments, in this early stage of therapy, on the feeling itself without any speculations as to origins.

The intrusive quality of some of Don's play is reinforced (Session 3) when he inserts a plastic hose (catheter?) into the gastank of a motorcycle, creating an "explosion." He soon shifts to elephant play, which also contains urethral representations with attention to the phallic-looking trunk. These two episodes constitute only a minor portion of a very active session otherwise devoted to feats of skill and competitions with adult father figures. T elects to emphasize the latter while waiting for more evidence before working on the more loaded urethral material.

In the next few sessions there is only a little play relevant to this theme: more attacks on the elephant's trunk; monkey puppets are given injections and don't like their red spectacle frames; and there is more dart shooting in the context of testing his skills in competition with apparent father figures.

Session 8 presents Don's first real preoccupation with "redness" and, predictably for him, this occurs in the context of a denial; that is, while drawing a picture of Bobo (whose most prominent feature is a large, red nose!). He delays doing the nose until last and comments that a nose would not really be red. (T misses a beautiful opportunity here to point out that it would be red if Bobo had a nosebleed.)

In the 10th session he plays out a dramatic sequence revealing castration fears and the infantile catheterization experience, as he repeatedly drops toy knives on the groin area of a figure constructed under the sand. T's comments increase in relevance from his hitting it in the middle where it hurts and makes a lot of blood, to describing the pain and helplessness of the victim. While his identification at first appears to be with the victim, toward the end of this prolonged episode he seems to be taking on the role of the aggressor. (T's notes after the session speculate that there may also have been considerable underlying guilt being expressed with respect to mother's miscarriages and hemorrhages; see further discussion under Theme IV.)

There is a marked retreat from these themes in the following session, but he returns to them again toward the end of Session 12, when he has an Indian jab spears into fish and a dinosaur, and the Indian is attacked in turn by a dinosaur–bull (father?) with large horns. The play then develops similarly to that of the 10th session, with knife attacks on figures buried in the sand. To T's inquiry as to whether Don has ever been cut with knives, he deflects the discussion to the cuts and injuries his brother has received. When T persists and inquires if he ever has seen his brother bleed, he again offers denials and excuses, but finally admits to having cut his own leg once. T then reflects on his difficulty in discussing such unpleasant things.

After another session of retreat from this theme, as Don works on overcoming his "sissy" image, the nosebleeds figure overtly and prominently in Sessions 14 and 15 in the context of Bobo. He draws a picture of Bobo's face (Session 14), then blackens out features as he shoots them on the actual Bobo, going from the eye, to the mouth (where he adds "blood dripping"), and finally to the threatening nose. But he only crosses out the nose without mentioning any blood. Thus he has displaced the "blood" from nose to mouth, and twice removed—from self to Bobo, to a picture of Bobo! In response to T's questions as to how he feels about blood, he now is able to admit that he has frequent nosebleeds. T then suggests that maybe his fear of nosebleeds keeps him from aggressively holding his own with his peers. He then moves to prepare Bobo for a facial operation, apparently as a cover-up excuse for attacking Bobo with knives, but he is unable to really carry through the "operation" (nosebleeds? T&A? or castration displaced upward?). He continues the nosebleed theme in Session 15 by hitting Bobo mainly on the nose; once he starts to wipe Bobo's "bloody nose" with his own tie, but quickly retreats. Later on he "kills" Bobo; another time he uses the stethoscope to see if he is still alive.

Three sessions later (18) Don plays out several episodes symbolic of urethral probes; pushing elongated balloons into the outstretched Slinky toy; poking darts into the balloons; again jabbing at balloons he has buried in the sand and calling this an operation; and tying an inflated long balloon to the easel so that it is erect, shooting at it with darts (after removing the rubber tips), then jabbing it with a knife until it burst.

The next four sessions contain no references to blood, but are devoted to tests of strength and skill, with many instances of his acting in a much more relaxed and spontaneous fashion. In Session 20, he creates a genital-looking contraption with two round balloons attached to the top of a bottle and spends much of the hour shooting at this until the balloons finally break (with the help of a pin). T comments on his trying to get it at exactly the right place. He returns to the blood theme, in Session 23, when he volunteers that Bobo is bleeding. When T asks about his own nosebleed now, he says he hasn't had as many lately and he's not afraid of them, just hopes they won't last long.

It is noteworthy that the climactic session in terms of Don's oedipal dilemma (see Session 24 in Theme IV) is introduced with the preparation of a bloody mixture he prepares as a treat for his invisible friend. References to blood and the blood theme are then carried into the first two of his four paintings.

The play starts with his mixing sand, water, soap, and red paint ("blood") into a Dr. Jekyll juice for his invisible friend. When the friend becomes suspicious, the brew is poured down the toilet which he calls an alligator (reminiscent of his first fascination with the red-mouthed alligator puppet in Session 2 which was fed a peppery, unpleasant mixture).

Don then proceeds to the first painting, announcing he is going to paint a "blood picture," and he does just that—big blobs of red (Figure 2). He agrees with T's comment that the red paint on the sheet of paper looks like blood would look on a bed sheet, then he indicates a (vague) face in the center of the redness. He points to an inverted U-shape, saying he doesn't know what that is; when T suggests a penis, he hurriedly turns the sheet over and starts the next painting. This is his invisible friend, and is a "she." He fills in the body area solidly with red "blood," huge quantities of it (Figure 3). He is not deterred by T's increasingly "bloody" comments (she's full of blood, it comes out of her nose, and out the other end, and gets all over everything) but continues in a totally absorbed manner to complete the picture. (The following painting relates exclusively to a house for his girlfriend and himself.) The fourth and final painting (Figure 5) is full of castration overtones with the blinded father–rival figure displaying huge, sharp teeth, good for cutting things off with (T's interpretation).

This session and its series of paintings proved to be the high point for the blood and castration themes as well as pinpointing his identification with his mother's hemorrhaging and miscarriages, which had been occurring through the same time period as his own nosebleeds.

In Session 26 Don looks to see if Bobo has been fixed "so it won't bleed" (leak sand), then hits him especially vigorously in the nose. The following session (27) he returns to mixing another brew, now called tomato juice, to which he adds red paint and starts to offer it to T. He panics when he spills some on the floor, runs for paper towels to soak it up, then disgustedly pours the rest down the toilet, exclaiming "Ugh" as he flushes away this menstrual-looking concoction. The discussion with T during his panic reveals his tendencies to handle guilt by masochistic self-injury as he confesses that he deliberately bites his lip to create blood to "cover" accidental spills of paint at home. T pursues the discussion in terms of his possibly seeing blood on the floor and wondering where it came from. Don ignores the implications, saying he only gets his hands bloody during a nosebleed attack.

This session (27) is the last in which Don's concerns about both sources of blood are brought up and, perhaps significantly, ushers in his demonstration in the next four sessions of his readiness to terminate: no longer dressing immaculately, feeling he can hold his own with his peers, and stating that he finally has achieved "self-confidence." There is one final reference to blood in Session 30 when he is philosophical about receiving a cut in a bike accident (just after passing his bike safety test!). Later in the session, when T is reviewing with him his progress in therapy, he at first denies he was ever really afraid of blood but adds that no one ever wants to get hurt; in other words, he is only human, too.

Theme IV. Oedipal Relationships to Mother

Mother figures and symbols are portrayed throughout the early sessions as "witchy," orally depriving, remote, and unfeeling. The normally expected oedipal fantasies appear to have been distorted due to pervading fears associated with mother's repeated pregnancies and miscarriages, as if it would be too dangerous for mother if she were to love any man or boy. The orally depriving aspects of mother figures overshadow any evidences of love and tenderness toward her sons. There is little ambivalence—rather, massive feelings of rejection and neglect.

The initial, but veiled, reference to oedipal themes occurs in Session 2 when, toward the end of the hour, the witch marries the alligator; this sequence ends with a theme of oral deprivation and death. In Session 3, after many sequences of rivalry with father figures in contests of strength and skill, and with only five minutes remaining, Don buries an apparent self-figure in the sand to sleep for fifty years. The figure is then lifted up while he says "Mother Angel" is calling him to her for fifty years.

In Session 5 concerns about multiple pregnancies occupy much of the hour and revolve around a witch figure and her two sons. The witch keeps having babies until she dies at the age of 355 with the request that the sons kill three of her enemies. The first two are readily eliminated but the sons are unable to vanquish the policeman (father figure?). Eventually they defeat a substitute figure, whereupon the witch–mother is resurrected and resumes the baby production. The two sons, as well as the "mother," keep repeating their fears that she will die, while T reflects the feelings children must have when their mothers are having babies. The two sons are joined by a third (an alligator, another self-figure?) who, although grown up, is a weakling and a crybaby; all three are barely fed by the stingy witch–mother. The alligator goes off on his own to find food and steals it from the General. The General–elephant–father arrives on the scene and is eliminated by the sons, creating a Pyrrhic victory since they are doomed to die and be replaced by two new sons. (Implicit in this theme of repeated pregnancies is the underlying belief that mother has not been pleased with her living sons; death as well as replacement are the fate of those children who have been a disappointment to her.)

Except for three minor references to mother figures, the next seven sessions are largely concerned with Don's struggles with such issues as evaluation by his peers (is he seen as a sissy?); more direct demonstrations of strength and skill; and further references to his dislike of dirt and blood. In Session 7 he makes a drawing of a witch (mother) who is chasing a drag racer (father). In Session 8, the skunk (his messy self) is repeatedly excluded from the house by various disapproving mother figures so that he must resort to sneaky tricks to steal cookie gratifications. The play scenes in Session 10 (discussed under Theme III in terms of blood and castration fears) in which he repeatedly jabs knives into the groin area of buried figures could also be seen as an acting-out of the insults to mother's body. (He may be feeling some guilt and responsibility for causing the miscarriages; for example, he may have upset her, or pushed against her stomach. In this connection, the dream he reported at the beginning of Session 4 gains relevance: a killer pushes against people with his whole body; Don had demonstrated by walking up to Bobo, who has a fat stomach, and pushing against him.)

The multiple-baby theme reappears in Session 13 with the magician not liking to have seven babies in the dollhouse, but this number quickly escalates to 21. In the final minutes of Session 16, the dangerous oedipal situation is enacted with the mother figure taking a dual role: (1) as a Queen more powerful (and desirable?) than the King, and (2) as the witch who is attacked by the devil (self?) with his horns. The all-powerful and castrating female then transforms the devil into a helpless little girl (sissy?).

In Session 17, the orally depriving mother is still objecting to her children sneaking cookies. In Session 19, the oedipal rivalry flares briefly in undisguised form when Don throws the mother doll on top of the father doll lying on a bed, and exclaims, "She goes to the father."

Four more sessions pass before Don returns to the oedipal theme with the dynamic and vigorous enactments of Session 24. Desire for the mother, rivalry with the father, castration anxiety, and fear of blood all coalesce in this climactic session. He initially assumes the good–bad mother role when he concocts a "delicious brew" of red paint ("blood") and sand for his "invisible" friend. (The designation of "Dr. Jekyll juice" for this drink immediately suggests to the therapist the dual nature of this symbolism.) The friend is suspicious of Don's good intentions and refuses the drink, whereupon he flushes it down the orally aggressive "alligator" toilet. He himself assumes a suspicious attitude with respect to the friend's now seemingly unwelcome return as he checks out the room for hidden entrances. T verbalizes his apparent fear that others (mother?) may be listening to his sessions, and emphasizes the privacy of his hour. With this reassurance he proceeds to paint four very red pictures.

The first painting (Figure 2) he calls a "blood picture." After T speculates on the similarity to the way the blood must look on his sheets after a nosebleed, he points to the form of a face, and then to a phallic shape, saying he doesn't know what that is. When T suggests it looks like a penis he quickly starts a new sheet. The next picture (Figure 3) is to be of his invisible friend, and he takes obvious pains to point out it is a "she" (since T had originally assumed and referred to the friend as "he"). When the face is completed and T comments that she looks sort of witchy, Don call her a "hag," but adds that he likes her very much, and also agrees with T's observations on his ambivalent feelings toward her (the good–bad mother). As he fills the body area with "blood," T draws the connection with his scary feelings toward nosebleeds, and to his mother's hemorrhages. With the addition of arms and legs he says she looks like a spider (a common symbol for the bad mother). T again points out that he really likes her in spite of her bloodiness and meanness.

In the next painting of a house (Figure 4), which is built in a swamp (impermanent foundation), the friend's bedroom is separated from Don's by the living room—an arrangement which T points out as making it difficult for him to reach her. Two interpretations are evident: (1) the wish to return to the womb where he could possess mother exclusively, and (2) the oedipal wish to supplant the father and have mother for himself, yet with the recognition that this would be impossible to attain. He then eats a cookie, saying that his girlfriend (mother?) will only give him one "poisoned" cookie. Not only is he orally deprived and punished for wanting to get too close, but also in retaliation for his earlier gift of the Dr. Jekyll juice which she had suspected was poisonous.

In the final painting of the series (Figure 5) he creates the figure of the "blind butler." This sightless father figure cannot see what is going on between Don and his lady friend, yet he can retaliate with his large, sharp teeth. (The oedipal situation is becoming dangerous: as the son, Don, is living with the mother and doesn't want the father–butler to "see" them, hence the blinding.) Don confesses that his girlfriend really likes the butler, and T points out his probable feelings of jealousy and frustration. He then takes T into his confidence with his "secret," that the butler is really her boyfriend, while he (Don) is the butler's father, thus reversing father–son roles and leaving himself in a safer position.

Identifying the butler as Don's son implies a series of reciprocal relationships: it is too painful to admit to mother's love for the butler as father; if the butler is portrayed as the boyfriend–son, he, in Don's place, can now safely express his affection for mother; Don, in turn, is thus removed to a safe distance to experience the father's perspective.

In the final direct confrontation via Bobo there is a series of dual displacements between father and son. If, at this point, the butler (Bobo) is still the son, then the beating by Don (as father) would be justified and deserved. But if the butler has reverted to representing the father figure, then Don's beating him becomes too threatening. The latter hypothesis seems to be confirmed in the next and final reversal of roles whereby the butler (now the father?) punishes Bobo (representing Don who has dared to assume father's place with mother).

The events of this session have seemingly brought to the surface and united many strands of Don's basic repressed conflicts: love of mother; fears for her safety; rivalry with father; and his fears of retribution via nosebleeds, damage, and castration. (From this point on through the remaining seven sessions, the referral problems show marked improvement as he demonstrates attributes of a normal boyhood: He soon appears in messy and patched clothes; he feels free to shoot the water pistol and mess in the sand; he displays more self-assurance and mastery; he is able to confide his secrets to T; and in the area of orality, he can not only accept cookies from T but spontaneously offers to share them with her.)

In Session 25, transference phenomena from mother to T are clearly evident as he portrays himself as T's son, is kidnapped by bank robbers, and pleads for T to rescue him. Earlier in this session Don has been T's young cousin, whose mother is portrayed as stingy with gum (in retaliation for the son's attacks on her); and there is a grandmother who doesn't want to see her own family. In the next session (26) Don continues the mother–therapist–son interactions, first reversing roles so that he, as the authority figure (policeman, fireman, phone operator), would deny T's requests and pleas for assistance. He then reverses roles again, as he asks T for foods and medical assistance. Shortly thereafter, he assumes the aggressor-resister stance as he comes near to shooting T with the water pistol.

In Session 27 he takes on the role of mother–provider and prepares some "tomato juice" (red paint) which he starts to offer to T, but it spills on the floor. His obvious panic after the spill probably was also its cause, if he feared T might actually drink the stuff. T's subsequent attempt to relate his disgust at the sight of the "bloody" water flushing down the toilet to other possible sources of blood is met by mumbling and denials.

Aside from one further sequence in Session 29, where T is instructed to, presumably, take the mother's role in making various phone calls for everyday kinds of requests, there are no further allusions to mother–son issues until the final session (31). Here Don becomes the provider, or good mother, as he prepares a pizza for the General (father). The crumbs would be given to the dog (self?). This leads to his final "secret," an experiment with sand and water which he works on in the lavatory out of T's sight. (This confirms T's belief that all of his secrets are somehow related to the mother–father–son complex of feelings.) He continues in the nurturant role as he then fills a baby bottle with an inflated balloon, "enough to last the baby all night," and ends the final session with a ceremonial farewell cake of sand for the therapist.

Additional Notes on the Role of the Witch

The most commonly agreed upon symbolism for the witch figure, in dreams, fairy tales, and children's play, is that of a bad-mother figure. Accoutred with her broom, long nose, and sharp teeth she becomes the feared, phallic, orally aggressive, and castrating symbol. When the role of the witch is followed in Don's fantasies, she figures initially as an orally depriving bad mother, while the castrating aspects are minimized. This apparently is a

function of the primacy of his earliest strong feelings of deprivation and affectional loss during infancy. Once these fundamen-
tal concerns have been mastered, the emphasis shifts to the more
typical witchy aspects relating to castration anxieties.

The witch appears initially in Session 2 and does not make
her final bow until the last (follow up) session. In Session 2 the
witch has powerful control over all the other characters. Three
witches look for, and fight over, a husband; one of them marries
the alligator (self-figure) in a seeming oedipal alliance, but the
play soon deteriorates with a theme of self-defeating maneuvers
whereby the ill-mated pair starve to death.

In Session 5 the witch is quite openly a mother figure, as
Don reenacts his mother's multiple pregnancies while her "sons"
fear for her life. In the end the witch–mother gives food to her
children, but only grudgingly.

In the drawing of a drag racer (Session 7), with its
masturbatory implications, the witch is depicted chasing the car.
This is the closest he comes to portraying her as a guilt-inducing
and disapproving figure.

In Session 16, the witch engages in a fight with the devil,
and reciprocally wards off attack from his sharp horns by
changing him into a girl—the ultimate castration. So the boy
(sissy) can blame the witch (mother) for his feminine qualities.
(This session comes four weeks after T first openly discussed the
issue of boys being called sissies but knowing they really are
boys.)

While painting the picture of his invisible friend (Session
24) Don accepts T's comment that she looks "witchy," and he
adds that she is a "hag." Nevertheless he protests that he likes
her. (She's all the mother he has!) The witch remains an active,
but unseen, force in this session when, after the next painting of
the girlfriend's (and his) house, he stops to eat the one and only
cookie allowed him by the (witchy) girlfriend, and a "poisoned"

one at that. That is the last mention of the witch until the follow-up session.

However, the themes of oral deprivation and grudging offers of food are continued in Session 25, but now in the context of imagined, but potentially real-life, characters such as cousins and cousins' mothers. In the follow-up session, Don assumes the role of provider of both good and bad food when he measures out sand, as food and as a witch's potion. (The witch's ghost cannot be laid to rest easily!)

Theme V. Rivalry and Identification with Father

Until the dramatic oedipal episode in Session 24 (discussed in detail in Theme IV), Don's play sequences involving father figures are clearly focused on contests of skill and the underdog's attempts to outwit and outmaneuver those who are stronger, more skillful, or more cunning, in a classical Adlerian portrayal of the son's attempts to achieve mastery over the father. This is not so much out of rivalry for mother's affections, but rather to emulate, and eventually replace, the father in a man's world.

Sessions 3 through 6 center largely on rivalry with an elephant (father figure) in which the weaklings usually are unsuccessful in winning various contests of strength and skill. (These play sequences also probably are revealing Don's feelings of being overpowered by his peers in his ineffectual efforts to compete with them.)

In Session 3, the self-figure does win most of the cycle and car races (father is a drag racer) culminating in the cycle (father's?) catching fire. Don puts the fire out with a fire hose, ending in a big "explosion." The self-figure then changes the cyclist into an elephant—a more overpowering figure. It cannot be changed back to a cyclist until it wins a fight with the self-figure. The contest is set up, not as a direct fight, but by hitting Bobo in a double-bind situation whereby the self-figure must not try to *not* defeat the elephant-father (in other words, the winning or losing must be genuine). Either the possibility of winning proves too threatening, or this back-handed way of overcoming the power figure is intriguing; in any case the self-figure's response is deliberately weak and so the elephant father remains immobilized. After T comments on his trying to act stupid as a means of controlling adults, he shifts immediately and has the self-figure defeat the elephant–father in a direct fight. Although the elephant loses this bout it is changed back into the cyclist anyway. T compliments the child figure for showing his real strength and not trying to pretend. Don celebrates the victory by giving each contestant a piece of cookie (and then eating these himself)—his first cookie-eating, but done in the context of rewards to father and son. (This session seems to encapsulate his rivalry with, and fear of, father's strength, for which his solution is to act weak and stupid. He also provides a clue as to the source of his learning difficulties at school; if he acts dumb and passive he will at least be safe.)

In Session 4, the Wolf-man figure (as self) successively defeats the elephant "Master" (by attacking his trunk), then the Lion–King of the desert, the President, the U.S. Army, and finally the King of the World. Unfortunately, none of these victims will befriend him, so he ends up turning his aggression inward and killing himself (again, it is too dangerous to challenge the father). In Session 5, after a long sequence in which the witch–mother undergoes repeated pregnancies, she is dying and asks her sons to eliminate her three enemies: a witch, some dinosaurs, and the policeman. The sons easily dispose of the first two, but the play disintegrates noticeably when the sons are fighting the policeman. Substitute father figures (soldiers) are introduced and defeated with one of them being called the policeman. Now the mother can be revived. Later in this session the alligator, a previous son of the witch but a weakling, does manage to eat a General's car, and the Wolf-man (self) succeeds in getting rid of the General, thus giving the sons free access to the witch–mother. The final minutes of this session and all of Session 6 are again focused on feats of skill with the darts. Don can vanquish lesser figures (soldiers, small animals) with evident pleasure and pride, but with the powerful figures of the elephant, the policeman, and one specific soldier, the sequences are set up in such a manner as to almost ensure defeat.

In Session 7 a fire station and a police station are side by side so that no one can tell where one leaves off and the other begins (identification to the point of losing identity). The officers end up by exchanging jobs, and the smaller cop guiltily confesses to putting out fires. A further merging of identities occurs when the small racer puts on the big racer's wheels (father's badge of distinction) but they fall off! The tragedy is rectified when a big "pusher" car helps the little car win the next race. Finally Don draws a picture of a huge driver in a racing car about to crash into a tree. (Does concern for father's safety hide a death wish?) The driver clasps the trunk of the tree to save the car; steam from the radiator and "mice" from a suitcase are pouring out of the vehicle. A witch (mother) is chasing after the racer while a menacing bat flies overhead. (The driver could be father or son, with sexual and/or masturbatory overtones; in either case the witch–mother obviously does not approve of the racer or the explosive climax.)

Two sessions (9 and 10) are preoccupied with shooting at, and finally defeating, powerful figures: a general, and a bull (Session 9), and the motorcycle cop, and a lion (Session 10). The entire Session 11 is taken up with the bull terrorizing the smaller animals, while Session 12 revolves around a rich man constructing and riding a magical rocket, and then cheating a poor man out of his money. The latter sequence involves role reversals and misrecognitions. When a horse lets two smaller and weaker figures (a chicken and a duck) ride on his back, they object when a man figure also wants to join them. (The children want mother to themselves without interference from father.) Finally, an Indian has to prove his identity and manliness by attacking small fish and dinosaurs, with a final battle against the horned bull-dinosaur. (Throughout these father–son episodes there are, of course, three interweaving threads: working through the oedipal conflicts with father, solving identity issues with respect to father, and achieving confidence and mastery in physical skills.)

The next three sessions (13,14,and 15) are largely devoted

to direct attacks on Bobo as Don works through his concerns about being regarded as a sissy and seeks to prove his prowess in order to establish a new relationship with his peers. Father figures reappear in Session 16 when the President and the General have their cars blown up by a group of army privates; later a group of wild animals kill each other with only the elephant surviving. Finally, in a series of good versus bad parental figures, the King is portrayed as being passive and less powerful than the Queen, and both watch as a second set of "evil" parent figures attack each other: the horned devil lunges at the witch, who, in retaliation, castrates him and changes him into a little girl. (The devil is obviously a double symbol at this point: the feared and envied father, whose sexual relations with mother are seen as an aggressive attack; and a naughty boy who desires the castrating mother, but she robs him of his manliness.)

There is another session (17) of vigorous, direct punching of Bobo, while Session 18 is clearly focused on phallic, masturbatory, and urethral symbolism which was elicited by the slinky toy and some long, red balloons.

The events of Session 19 are noteworthy in view of the fact that Don's father had accompanied his mother to her session on this day. Early in the hour Don draws two animals, an elephant and an alligator, each with phallic-like appendages (see Figure 1). He becomes quite uneasy when T comments on the things hanging down. He immediately sets up darts, as traffic signs, in the sand and has the motorcycle cop knock them all over without realizing what he is doing. (The unconscious is pretty powerful!) Toward the end of this same session he throws the dollhouse father onto the bed, and then the mother on top of him, saying, "She goes to the father." (Has the concurrent joint session for his parents reinforced his jealousy of his father and confirmed his feelings of being ineffective and weak?) This leads to the final scene of a baby carriage that tries to do everything the big cars do; the audience taunts the carriage to go back to its bottle. But the carriage sticks with it and is finally accepted by the car drivers (fathers) and even paid a large sum of money to join them.

Don seems quiet and subdued in the initial portion of the next session (20), which followed father's visit to the clinic. (Is he wondering whether T might mention it or question him about his reactions?) After a sequence with little play figures who are forgetful and ineffective, he spends the rest of the hour with the balloons. He puts his rat-finks in a bottle and shoots over their heads, saying the rat-finks are uneasy and don't realize this is all for their own good. (Parental explanations for the need for therapy?)

In the second session after father's visit, a father figure has been told there has been a change in his son and rushes to the hospital. (The clinic is in a hospital.) Father assumes it is bad news, while actually the son is getting better. (Does father always expect the worst, or find it impossible to recognize improvement?) In Session 22, the small King Kong is compared in size to the elephant and the dog and is put on a throne. His subjects try in every way to please him with offerings of food and furniture but he is never satisfied. (Another instance of not being able to please father or to take his place.) In Session 23, after T observes that he is getting rid of his baby ways, Don relates with pride his successes when target shooting with his father and older brother. When his darts hit the mark, he says he can't wait to tell his mother, but demurs when T asks whether father would not also be pleased.

The complete oedipal drama is acted out in Session 24 via the four red paintings, starting with his affection for his "invisible friend" (mother), and ending with aggressive attacks on, and from, the "blind butler" (father). Initially T assumes that Don is the butler, blinded, as was Oedipus, for loving his mother (encompassing the wish and its denial). He quickly lets T know that the butler is a new boyfriend of his girlfriend. When T comments that he (Don) must feel very jealous and want to keep them apart, he makes the disclosure that he is the butler's father. (This reversal of father and son identities removes himself from the oedipal triangle as he yields to the father.) Finally, he engages in direct attacks on Bobo who is the butler (son? father?) then initiates another role reversal with Bobo becoming Don whom he then beats up while taking the part of the butler. Seemingly now the son is punished for his oedipal desires.

In the next five sessions (25–28) Don seems preoccupied with explorations of the meaning and purpose of therapy and of his ambivalent, dependent–independent relationship to the therapist. There are overtones of transference reactions, mild resistances, and feigned attacks on T, and three instances of symbolic self-injury in one session (27).

About this time (Session 29), father comes in for another joint session with mother's therapist; there is no noticeable effect on Don's behavior this time. However, after a two-week lapse over spring vacation, there is reference to father (Session 30) in connection with the report of a bike accident Don had had only three hours after passing a safety test. He spontaneously reports father's sarcastic comment, "Some safety!", and does not seem too upset about it; joking comments from his peers had not bothered him at all. Later in the hour he talks about the teacher's phone call to tell his mother how well he is doing, and elaborates on how happy this made both his mother and himself; he is very noncommittal when T asks if father was happy too.

There is one allusion to the all-powerful father figure in the final session (31). Don assumes the role of meting out gratifications, and these are specifically for the General, with only the crumbs to go to the dog (self?). Has he accepted the fact that he cannot supplant father, or are these matters still unresolved?

Theme VI. Masturbatory Fantasies

The first apparent representations of any masturbatory impulses or concerns do not occur until almost two months into therapy, and only infrequently thereafter until Session 18 and beyond. The first six sessions are largely devoted to themes of rivalry with father figures in contests of strength and skill or by outwitting them with underhanded maneuvers of sneakiness and misrepresentation; a second theme of these early sessions relates to orally depriving mother symbols. In Session 4, after relating a scary dream of a killer who pushes against people with his whole body, Don demonstrates by walking up to Bobo and pushing against him. He then spends some time in attacking the rubber elephant, especially on its trunk, or by holding the trunk and flipping the animal over.

In Session 7, with the fire station and police station located side-by-side, the smaller motorcycle cop assumes the role of the larger fireman and starts to put out a fire. Everything gets very wet (ejaculation or enuresis?) so that the smaller cop sinks into the sandy ground with only his head showing above the sand (bed covers?). The big fire chief–father mistakes him for a statue (erection?) and the little cop confesses he was putting out the fires (in imitation of father). Don then carefully and meticulously brushes the wet sand off the toy and washes it in the sink (guilt and restitution). It is also at the end of this session that he draws a racer in a car, with clear masturbatory symbolism: the racer's long arm reaches out to clasp the trunk of a tree, with his fingers touching a hole in the trunk; steam comes out of the radiator; and a witch–mother chases after the racer (scolding and/or spying?).

Session 9 marks Don's first use of the water pistol with its erotic and urethral connotations. The outstanding aspect of this initial use is his overcontrol and concern about getting any water on the table and wall.

Early in Session 12 masturbatory fantasies are prominent in the sequence of a rich man's rocket that could go in the air and underwater. The pilot forgets to punch the button to deflate the wings when it hits the water, so everything gets wet! The pilot is punished by being sent to jail (resolution of guilt).

There is little reference to this theme during the next five sessions, which are concentrated on vigorous pummeling of Bobo, as he works through his concerns about being a sissy and his desire to compete with his peers. In Session 18 the introduction of a small spiral Slinky toy generates considerable activity; Don stretches it to its full length, and stuffs inflated long balloons inside. Then he concentrates on the long balloons, filling them with water, blowing them up and jabbing them with knives, using them as cigars, and shooting them with darts.

In Session 19 Don produces two animal drawings (Figure 1) with phallic appendages, resulting in a play disruption when T's comments become too direct for him to tolerate at this point. His anxiety is expressed in his next play in which a motorcycle cop knocks over all the traffic signs without realizing what he is doing, thus doing all the things the signs were warning against. (It is important to "pay attention" and be vigilant in order not to reveal one's unconscious fantasies and preoccupations.)

Session 20 marks the high point of symbolic representation of the masturbatory theme. Don puts two small rat-fink toys in the baby bottle and affixes two round balloons on either side of the bottle under the cap. He then balances this genital-looking contraption precariously on top of the easel. Most of the hour is spent in trying to shoot, and burst, the balloons. When the construction falls off, he ends up under the easel and continues to shoot at it and to jab it with the pin of a badge, while commenting that the rat-finks don't realize this is all for their own good. After casually jabbing a dart at Bobo's buttocks as he passes by him, he futilely tries to blow up the torn balloons, saying they are no good now (guilt?). He seems relieved when T recognizes his worries.

In the first of the series of red paintings in Session 24 (see Figure 2), he points to an inverted U-shape and says he doesn't know what it is. T's speculation that it looks like a penis again is too much for him and he goes on to the next painting. The next six sessions revolve around issues of the good versus bad mother, freer use of the water pistol, and verbal expressions of his sense of emergent self-competence.

In the final session (31) Don returns to the balloon–bottle play with its overtones of masturbatory concerns. His sand and water "experiment" in the baby bottle involves a "secret formula," which he works on in the lavatory out of sight of T; he is philosophical about his lack of success. Then he blows up a long red balloon which he puts in the bottle so that it extends and looks like an appendage to the bottle. As he keeps squeezing the balloon to expand and then deflate it, he says, "It's enough to last the baby all night" (thus acting out the night's secret activities?). This speculation is confirmed as he gingerly digs the now damp and deflated balloon out of the bottle and drops it in the wastebasket. In the next sequence he sticks an inflated balloon through the rim of toy eyeglasses and puts them on, but says it doesn't look like him. (He can't believe he can really engage in these activities?)

NOTE: Of all the themes discussed in this section, it would seem that this one was the least fully worked through in the course of the thirty-two sessions, since Don seemed to be just beginning to feel free enough to play out conflicts in this area. Whether such concerns on his part were major enough to have justified continuation of therapy for further exploration, or whether these were part of the normal development to be expected at his age, is a moot question. The therapist leaned toward the latter view, feeling that Don's progress in other areas had freed him up enough to be able to recognize and deal with these hitherto unmentionable impulses at his own pace.

Theme VII. From Oral Deprivation to Gratification

Overview

The subject to be traced in this theme is only secondarily concerned with the symbolic significance of play acts portraying aspects of oral deprivations from infancy onward; these have been covered in the discussions under Theme IV (Oedipal Relationships to Mother). Rather, the emphasis here is to follow the child's actual behavior when confronted with real food in the sessions, and to determine how this behavior is related to, or parallels, the more dynamic aspects of play symbolism. In effect, the refusals and acceptances of food, and the uses to which it is put in each hour can serve as a barometer of general progress in the play sessions.

This "cookie" strand begins with Don's view of a bad-mother figure who niggardly, if at all, condescends to feed her children (while he ignores the actual cookies set before him). He moves from sessions where he eats them only via proxies (the play food has to be disposed of somehow!), to open indulgence of his oral hungers, to his recognition that the therapist herself might also be hungry. Finally, he becomes the provider of food, first grudgingly and under a cloud of suspicion to be sure, but terminating with his farewell gift of a sand-cake to the therapist in his final session.

Don's reactions to food can be grouped rather neatly within each quarterly period of therapy. During the first two months (Sessions 1–8), the focus is on symbolic themes of oral deprivation on the part of mother figures and on the evil aspects of food. There are numerous incidents of self-denial on his part when he does finally build up enough courage to approach the goodies. Toward the end of this time-frame he is able to help himself directly. During the second "quarter," any mention of food or use of food is noticeably absent.

The third two-month period (Sessions 17–24) starts out with a "loaded" session (17) filled with strong orally aggressive and cannibalistic themes, and references to the orally depriving mother, but ends on his most positive cookie reaction to date as he laughingly takes "one for the road." Sessions 18–23 are totally positive with the cookies obviously serving as a comforting device. Then comes the climactic 24th session that commences with the good–bad Dr. Jekyll juice that, in turn, serves to introduce the subsequent portrayal of the classical oedipal triangle.

During the final quarter (Sessions 25–31), Don at last offers a cookie to the therapist, albeit quickly reverting to a play dialogue which puts himself in the position of the depriver. Positive aspects toward food continue on through the final session (31) where he offers the therapist a farewell sand-cake. In the follow-up session two months later, the hour is spent in making sand dishes, first as food but finally as a witch's brew—ambivalence is still present.

Session by Session

Vanilla wafers were always in the room beginning with Session 2. T points them out to Don and assures him he can have all he wants, but he listens impassively. After several sequences with various puppet figures, his first food theme appears with the monkey making an imaginary spicy-hot brew that he pours down the alligator's mouth. T points out that what looked like good food actually turns out to be bad. When told there are only five minutes left in this session, he casually glances toward the cookies. This seems to trigger a play sequence of oral deprivations and the denial of the wish to be fed: the puppets can't find any real food and so are forced to eat the wastebasket and the clock (thus denying the passage of the hour), and finally the refrigerator, with the rationalized denial, "so if they did find some food there won't be any place to keep it." T tries to verbalize his ambivalence and hesitation which only yields a further open denial on his part to the effect that he never really gets hungry.

It is noteworthy that, after having seemingly ignored the cookies during their initial presentation in Session 2, while playing out themes of self-denial and starvation, in the following session (3) he brings in a plastic *skeleton*, which serves as his identification figure throughout the session. (Has the implied starvation been imposed by others or is it self-inflicted?) He does mention that he had traded (given up) one of his two plastic hot dogs for the toy. In the early play sequences he represses any oral activity while engaging Skelly in various contests of strength and skill. Eventually, the cookie temptation becomes too great, but he can yield only in the context of having his play figures "eat" the cookies as rewards. (The broken-up bits of cookie then must be disposed of by his eating them.) In the next sequence Skelly will only agree to stay in the General's house on condition that he can have all the cookies he wants (thus providing a rationale for indulging, albeit still vicariously). This proxie cookie-eater reluctantly gives a small piece of cookie to a friend, who doesn't appreciate it, crumbles it up on the floor, and then hides the mess under the bed. This orgy of oral indulgence, and unwillingness to share his goodies, culminates in Skelly's self-inflicted death and burial as punishment for giving in to his oral cravings. In the final minutes of the hour, Skelly is magically rescued by "Mother Angel" (the wished-for giving mother) and carried up to heaven.

As if in reaction to his boldness and revelations in the previous session, in Session 4 Don talks some about food for the play figures but does not have them eat any. The early play themes of Session 5 center on the witch–mother's numerous pregnancies. There are also scenes in which her sons are hungry, and are only niggardly given half-cookies (which Don eats for them). The alligator, in defiance, goes out to hunt food for himself (he's building up courage) and returns to report he ate the General's car. Again, with only five minutes left, Don launches into an orgy of cookie eating under the guise of animals being well fed at the zoo. The deprivation then reappears when the animals are transferred to the circus and given only water. When the elephant leaves to find peanuts, the camel hurries to finish all the cookies and gorges until he is feeble and sick and finally dies from (guilty) self-indulgence (repeating Skelly's fate in Session 3).

It is not until Session 6 that Don can eat cookies directly, in his own name as it were, rather than through a proxy. Also, for the first time he clearly shows genuine pleasure in his skill with the dart gun, seems more at ease, and acts in a more self-confident manner. Once, in reaching for a dart, his hand comes near the cookie jar; he calls this to T's attention. Soon he becomes bolder and openly eats the cookies, but only three in all. Cookies could only be eaten as a consolation prize if he misses a shot; since he is proving quite skillful at darts, he thus limits the extent of his oral gratification. He encapsulates his ambivalence: he wants them yet feels guilty in doing so.

Session 8 is notable as the first time he eats all of the available cookies, but this is not until late in the session and through a proxy. Earlier in this hour, as he is reaching for the crayons, he seemingly puts his hand in the cookie jar accidentally and exclaims, "Oops, the wrong thing." His self-denial is still strong even though T encourages him to take some. In the final play theme, the skunk (child) sneaks into the alligator's (parent's) house and gobbles up all the cookies. The alligator is cross because all the food is gone—so guilt is relieved by disapproval from the depriving parent.

There are no recorded instances of the use of cookies in the next seven sessions (9–15). It is of course possible that because of his progress in this area such usage was taken for granted by

T and no longer noted. (If, in fact, he did not resort to cookie eating this may indicate that once he developed enough self-assurance and courage to unself-consciously clean out the bowl, he no longer felt the need for reassurance through oral channels.) This was a period when he was working through concerns around operations and castration fears, becoming more aggressive with Bobo, and preoccupied with the sissy themes and identity issues. In Session 16 he wistfully discusses Christmas, which had not turned out too well; celebration of his Christmas Eve birthday is being delayed (either by his parents or his own wishes?), and he has forgotten to bring in the birthday card T had sent him. At this point, he does reach for a cookie (as a comforting device?).

Oral themes reappear in various guises during the third quarter of therapy (Sessions 17–24). Session 17 is particularly loaded with oral- aggressive and oral-incorporative aspects. After thirty minutes of very aggressive pummeling of Bobo, Don threatens to eat him, pretends to slice him up and devour him, but he doesn't taste good. The skunk offers a steak as a reward to the dog if he will clean house for him; the alligator eats two people as well as the skunk. Noticing only five minutes remaining, Don reaches for a cookie saying, "One for the road," and laughs as he eats it. This was followed by a reference, in brief doll play, to the mother objecting to her kids sneaking cookies; in response to T's question he admits that his mother is that way too. As he leaves the room he takes another cookie and was obviously pleased when T's "One for the road" signals her recognition and approval of his first attempt to take a cookie on leaving. (This phrase is to become a sort of secret joke between C and T in subsequent sessions—a bond of mutual understanding and rapport between them.)

In Session 18, after considerable play with Bobo, with obvious attendant feelings of competence and self-assurance, he engages in quite phallic-looking play with the slinky, pushing a long balloon through it and eating a cookie when he finishes.

This is followed by a much longer play sequence with the balloons, filling them with water, blowing them up, and shooting them with darts. When the hour is up he starts to leave, comes back for a cookie, leaves again, and comes back a second time for oral supplies. He smiles in agreement when T comments on his needing enough to last him until the next session.

Don eats several cookies during Session 19 as he plays at competitive contests between a baby carriage and big cars amid taunts from the latter that the baby should go back to its bottle (mother?). He leaves this session in an animated mood, taking a cookie "for the road." This is the first time he says "Goodbye" to T; he is now feeling much more "at home" in therapy and with the therapist. His first actual play with the baby bottle occurs in Session 20 when he incorporates it into what becomes a genital-looking construction which he uses as a dart target. Again, on leaving, he takes "one for the road." There is only brief mention of food in Session 22 as he pours sand ("food") over King Kong. In Session 23 he sets up animals and the baby bottle as targets for his dart play, interspersing these episodes with vigorous punches at Bobo. T's comparisons of his little brother using the bottle versus Don's no longer doing babyish things with it releases a flood of boasting about his prowess and even more energetic play with Bobo. When the hour is up he is reluctant to leave, shoots one more dart, and helps himself to a cookie.

The dramatic 24th session opens with more dart shooting at the baby bottle and further observations by T that he seems to be outgrowing his former babyish, sissified behaviors. He then uses a small medicine bottle (rather than the larger baby bottle) to mix his Dr. Jekyll juice (red paint, soap, and sand) as a delicious brew for his invisible friend. The latter becomes suspicious of his intent, giving T the opportunity to explore the primitive, ambivalent good–bad aspects of food with the attendant fears of being poisoned by a bad mother. Don continues in the oral–incorporative vein as he pours the juice down the alligator's (bad son's) mouth and flushes it down the toilet in "one big gulp." His suspiciousness remains as he searches the room for his invisible friend who might have sneaked back in. T's reassurance that no one (i.e., mother) can come in or overhear them reaffirms the confidentiality of the hour and unleashes the series of four vivid paintings depicting the classic oedipal struggle. After the painting of the house (Figure 4) which defines the inaccessibility of his girlfriend, he eats one "poisoned" cookie, saying his girlfriend (the orally depriving mother) will only let him have one. (The interrelationships of the various play themes in this session—suspicions and poisonings in the context of the girl friend–mother—lend credence to one of the postulated origins of the paranoid position as originating in early oral deprivations and fantasies that mother's food is too dangerous to eat.)

The final quarter of therapy commenced with Don's first offer of a cookie to T (Session 25), indicating that he has arrived at the point where his self-absorption has abated to the extent that he now becomes more aware of, and attuned to, the world around him.

This bold, for him, reaching out can only be done in a once-removed semi-depriving context by directing T to phone him and ask to buy a cookie from him. After giving her the first one, he keeps raising the price on her subsequent calls, and only pretends to give the cookies to her. A play disruption occurs when T attempts to relate the play to his own possible experiences of not ever getting all he wants. He soon recovers and takes the part of T's baby cousin who complains that his mother won't give him even one piece of bubble gum. Keeping the play in a family once-removed enables T to talk about the cousin's stingy, orally depriving mother. Don responds that the cousin is afraid his mother will hear them talking. (Again, as in the previous session, the theme of mother's deprivations brings up his reality fear that his own mother can overhear, or become aware of, what they are discussing in therapy. Oral deprivation is a very basic and symbolic life-threatening situation for him, and, ipso facto, the crux of his difficulties.) Don then rationalizes the restrictions of the cousin's mother as being punishment for the cousin's acting-out behavior. In the final play scene, Don becomes T's son (the first and only instance) who is being devoured by a dangerous fish (the bad mother?). T rushes to the rescue, and he helps himself to a cookie as he leaves.

The food aspects of Session 26 involve imaginary orgies of oral gratification as T is directed to play the grocer and fill his mammoth phone orders for food; but he must disguise his own oral longings—the food is not for himself but for the farmer's cow! During this and subsequent play he keeps eating cookies and feels free enough to take the remaining three cookies in the bowl as he leaves, while calling T's attention to his boldness. In Session 27 he plays the part of a cook and prepares tomato juice (again red paint, soap, and sand) which he offers to T, but he panics and terminates the play when he spills a few drops on the floor.

No more references to food occur until what he has decided is to be his last session (31). After some hard jousting matches with Bobo he makes a sand pizza for the General; only the crumbs will be given to the dog. When T sympathizes with the underdog he becomes more generous. A water and sand mixture in the baby bottle becomes a "secret experiment" that fails; at least he's trying more adult activities. The bottle then becomes a receptacle for a long red balloon in a replay of earlier phallic symbolism, with either bottle and/or the balloon being "enough to last the baby all night" (a symbol with dual meaning, both oral and masturbatory gratification). When the hour is up he closes the session by making "one last cake" of sand, and writing "Goodbye" on it as his nonverbal farewell.

The follow-up session two months later is almost completely devoted to oral themes. Although Don more or less "reviews" all his previous play activities in his initial cursory inspection of all the play equipment, he settles finally on sand play, making dishes of food, and, lastly, a witch's brew (the good and bad aspects of food are thus highlighted once more). He makes no mention of the cookies this time, nor does he eat any of them.

Chapter 4

The Therapeutic Process and the Role of the Therapist

Introduction

In going through the sessions one final time the emphasis now will focus on the therapist and her role as commentator–interpreter, with exploration of the apparent effect of her verbalizations on Don's immediate and subsequent behavior. In retrospect, the therapist was originally perceived by Don more or less as a hostess, the provider of a place to play, and someone who perhaps talked too much. Only in the latter third of the sessions (from about Session 19) did he feel free enough to test the limits of the room and to express his concerns for privacy and confidentiality. From here he moved to seeing the therapist as a separate person in her own right (while at the same time expressing transference wishes of exchanging therapist for mother). In short, he finally feels "at home" with the therapist. It was as if only after gaining some realization of his own progression from a fearful and timid weakling to a lad with self-confidence and self-assurance could he begin to explore the framework of therapy itself.

181

In the process notes, those therapist–child interactions were recorded which stood out as unusually meaningful or that seemed, at the time, to be memorable milestones or possible preludes to future directions. However, the therapist did not remain inactive or passive, rather she made running comments and interpretations throughout the sessions with respect to the activities being played out. For example, in the early sessions she kept pointing out his constantly recurring need to rationalize or to excuse his constricted behavior. Whenever it seemed appropriate she speculated on what he must be feeling, and later, because he could more freely express himself, she would emphasize and label his feelings for him.

Sessions 1–32

Session 1

As an introduction to the first session, T provides an explanation of the structure of the sessions and, after asking if Don knows why he is coming, she offers further clarification. His initial behavior with the darts clearly reflects his compulsive, careful, and emotionless approach to any new situation. T's comments to the effect that he doesn't seem especially pleased or angry with his successes and failures seem to loosen him up a bit. He volunteers information about his mother's supervision and restrictions on his play, in effect calling attention to his unease at the freedoms he senses in this new setting. When the hour is up, T is careful to repeat her structuring of the sessions: that he would be coming every week, and that everything would be kept confidential between him and T. She establishes some measure of rapport with her comment that this must seem quite different from anything he's ever done before. Nevertheless he keeps his distance from T as they leave the playroom.

Session 2

Cookies are introduced for the first time and T makes a point of indicating their presence and purpose—he can have all he wants. He makes no response and devotes the time to puppet play. This is the first of many metaphorical sequences that appear throughout the first 18 or 20 sessions. As Ekstein (1966) points out:

> The metaphor utilizes primary-process material, manipulates it, as it were, but does not translate or lift its meaning into the language of the secondary process. . . . The use of the metaphor serves the defensive function of allowing the patient to maintain greater distance from conscious awareness of the content of the conflict, even while serving the adaptive functions of facilitating a reduction in distance between the therapist and the patient [p. 159].

T gradually moves from running commentary on the activities going on, to observations about the puppet characters (as when the alligator gets his mouth burned, or the witch's curious sense of values relative to the importance of various rooms), to finally pointing out Don's own inner conflict between wanting to let go and be messy, and feeling guilty when these urges do break through. She then tries to explain what guilty feelings must be like. Don slightly agrees to all of this, which indicates to T that such interpretations so early in the process will not lead to withdrawal on his part.

With five minutes left, Don rather casually glances at the cookie jar, then plays out a drama where characters are hungry for "real" food yet are forced to engage in self-defeating maneuvers and eventually starve to death. T suggests perhaps he would like to have some cookies, just as the puppet figures wanted real food, but maybe he feels uncomfortable about taking any. She elects not to pursue his denial that he ever gets hungry, but assures him that they will always be there for him.

Session 3

Themes of messiness and dirt are prominent and T continues to point out his tendencies to rationalize or deny his dislike of the sand in particular and dirtiness in general. Later in this session Don has his little Skelly (self?) figure deliberately act dumb when in physical competition with the elephant. Here T's initial comments probably miss the mark, as she is seeing the episode in terms of a possible cause of Don's learning difficulties in school; namely, that Skelly was taking a negativistic or defeatist position by trying to play dumb in order to control grown-ups. However it seems more likely that this was an instance of father–son conflict, with the smaller figure being afraid to come out as the winner.

But all is not lost, and in the next Skelly episode T can retrieve her error as she then interprets the play more in terms of the son's attempt to defeat the father figure. Confirmation of this view is revealed as Don immediately starts eating cookies for the first time (albeit by proxy) in the context of rewards to each contestant.

During the remainder of the session, the significance of the skeleton becomes apparent as he has this emaciated figure engage in a frenzied bout of cookie eating. Guilt soon takes over as Skelly buries himself in the sand, only to be rescued (forgiven?) and reclaimed by the Mother Angel.

Session 4

Themes of rivalry with the elephant (father) were continued from the previous session. Victory over him does not satisfy, so that more and more powerful figures become the targets of attack, but none of these victories brings real satisfaction or admiration from the populace.

Session 5

When they enter the room T places a "Do Not Disturb" sign on the door and explains it in terms of maintaining the privacy of Don's hour. In talking about his big brother, Don is able to verbalize several annoying incidents that had made him angry, but says he doesn't dare show it. T elaborates on his probable feelings and that it must be hard to hold it all in.

The first clear references to his mother's multiple pregnancies occurs in this session in terms of a witch who has repeated pregnancies while her two sons are fearful she might die. T keeps her reflections in the context of the witch and the witch's sons and how awful they must feel each time she is having another baby.

The witch–mother also proves to be orally depriving, which soon leads to a final episode of Don's gorging on cookies (via the zoo animals) and T's running commentary on how good it is to have all they want.

Session 6

A water pistol was introduced in order to stimulate play around urethral concerns. Don tells of "accidentally" getting his friend wet with one. T proposes that maybe he was pleased with himself and pursues his denials until he finally admits it was funny. (He does not actually use the water pistol until Session 9.)

His subsequent successes in dart play are repeatedly reinforced by T's comments until he finally volunteers that he is having fun—a real concession for this reserved and constricted child. With this gain in self-confidence he finds the courage to take cookies directly (rather than by proxy) for the first time. In essence, as he gains more self-assurance in his own skills, he also feels less self-conscious in the playroom and with T.

On leaving the room he brushes off his pants; T asks if he is afraid his mother will scold and guesses that he really is worried about that.

Session 7

Even with T's prodding, Don has trouble admitting to feeling bad when his older brother was given more privileges than he on a recent hunting trip.

Later in this session, as he washes sand off a toy, T poses both sides of his ambivalence: is he afraid he might be scolded, or does he really not like to have things be dirty? He denies and rationalizes in terms of what "the other kids" would think if they found dirty toys. This leads, perhaps too quickly, to T's probing his reactions to her also seeing other children, thus sidelining for the time being the real issue of his cleanliness concerns.

While drawing a picture of a racing car and driver, Don identifies the various characters. Since the interface of the driver and the tree trunk strongly suggests masturbatory symbolism, T focuses her comments on the manual activities as portrayed (but without actually labeling her specific speculations) rather than probing for any explanations of characters and details. To do the latter might have stifled his sudden creativity.

Session 8

When Don remarks that he can draw better than his brother, T again seizes the opportunity to confront him with the denials and excuses he usually gives to cover his feelings of inferiority to his brother. She speculates that he must feel bad and disappointed much of the time. Later on, T misses the first real opening she has had to make direct reference to his nosebleeds. Don is drawing the Bobo character, who has a very large, round, and red nose. He waits to draw the nose until last, and remarks that it really wouldn't be red. He thus avoids and then denies the redness and T falls into the trap of also avoiding this crucial subject!

(Fortunately, such missed opportunities can usually be retrieved because they will reappear, see Sessions 14 and 15, if not resolved initially. However, one cannot "miss the boat" too many times or the child will drop the subject permanently.)

Session 9

The denials and excuses surface again when T encourages Don to use the water pistol while he is showing some interest by fingering it. (It has been in the room for the past three sessions.) When T suggests he try it, he starts giving reasons for not doing so, but T reminds him of earlier episodes when he has used excuses to hide his real interests and desires. This seems to give him enough reassurance so that he spends considerable time with the gun, albeit in a methodical shooting game with the target toys carefully laid out on a plastic table covering! T's comments focus on his not needing to be so careful here and that this must seem a strange place in that he doesn't get scolded for these things.

The end of this session elicits further structuring of the playroom as a place that other children and other doctors also use, since he wants to put his toys where he could find them next week. He accepts her explanation.

Session 10

Don keeps looking for difficult targets for the darts and T reflects on his evident pleasure when he succeeds. There is an opportunity later in this session, as he is jabbing knives into a constructed figure buried in the sand, for T to introduce the concept of blood and the figure's uneasiness at not knowing when or where it would be hurt next. In suggesting where it was being hit, she deliberately adds "middle" and "bottom" to the usual arms, legs, and so on. He agrees to the fear and the hurt and that he is aiming for the "middle."

T senses that, in addition to the apparent reenactment of his traumatic urethral insults as an infant, he is also identifying with mother and reliving her miscarriage experiences. (Does he in some way feel responsible?) However, T only goes as far as emphasizing the possible bloodiness in the middle area—viewing the symbolic play as covering either or both contingencies.

Session 11

As so often happens, a very dynamic or "loaded" session is followed by a degree of retreat, as if the child is aware that he has revealed too much. Nevertheless, the metaphor was readily apparent—with the bull (father) attacking smaller animals and becoming particularly ferocious with those in a baby carriage. Is father also seen as responsible for mother's miscarriages? Is this what men and boys are in danger of doing to women? (Although T has called the vehicle a baby "carriage" in her process notes, and afterwards made the analogy to a *miscarriage*, there is no indication from the notes whether Don had actually used this term.)

Session 12

In a series of enactments, play figures pretend to be somebody else or to do impossible things. Don accepts T's comments to this effect.

The next sequence involves small animals riding on a horse's back but they object to letting a man get up with them. Here, T's remark that "it looks like the kids don't want the father around" is much too direct and results in a play disruption; he immediately puts these toys back on the shelf.

Then he brings out a new set of animals and repeats the initial theme of characters not following their prescribed roles. Now T further elaborates on her earlier comments (to the first sequence) and extends the analogy to embrace the issue of sex identity; boys sometimes wishing they were girls, or being called sissies yet knowing they really are boys. As so often in these sessions, when T seems to have hit upon a crucial issue, Don makes little response except possibly smiling to himself or, as in this instance, nodding quietly.

He then reintroduced the jabbing play (begun in Session 10) and T pursues the earlier theme of bleeding, asking if he has ever been cut. He denies, as usual, and discusses cuts his brother has received. As T pursues his tendency to deflect or deny unpleasant things, he finally admits to having once cut his leg. T summarizes by letting him know that she realizes how difficult it is for him to talk about these things.

With only five minutes remaining, Don looks longingly at the new dart gun but says there isn't enough time to use it. T challenges his tendencies to deny his real wishes and suggests he could do a lot in five minutes. Thus supported and reinforced, he does spend the remaining time with the gun.

Session 13

Don returns to the "sissy" theme of last session's play, using a figure he has brought from home. It is a small robed priest (thus a man in feminine-looking clothes) who demonstrates his remarkable skills and objects to being called such things as a "weakling." When T adds the concept of "sissy," Don quickly adds this to the list of derogatory adjectives. T, with her comments, keeps reinforcing the strengths of this figure and his happiness at being accepted. This encouragement leads to Don's hitting and beating on Bobo directly, for the first time, rather than with darts or toy animals. He even verbalizes, "Don't you call me a sissy," as he has the priest alternately beat Bobo with mild or strong strokes. With T's repeated cheering from the sidelines he expresses the wish that Bobo were really his brother, so that he could beat him up.

Session 14

Don's rationalizations in the face of disappointment appear early in the session with his discussion of the brief time his father would allow their Christmas tree to be up; T verbalizes his probable wish to have it up longer.

He moves to more vigorous and direct punching of Bobo, then draws a picture of Bobo's face and blackens out each feature as he hits it with the darts: first an eye; then the mouth as he talks about "blood dripping"; then the nose which he only marks out with an X. Here T recovers from her earlier omission in Session 8; she comments on the bloody mouth and asks how he feels about blood. He makes no response immediately, but as he returns to direct hitting of Bobo he brings up the subject of nosebleeds for the first time, volunteering that he used to have frequent nosebleeds, and had one the previous week. T suggests maybe he's afraid to fight the other boys for fear of getting a nosebleed. He then proposes to give Bobo an operation but never quite goes through with it.

Session 15

The first portion of this session continues the references to Bobo's bloody nose—now a topic that can be discussed more easily and openly. Eventually he "kills" Bobo, then makes restitution by giving him a lot of money. T points out his feelings of guilt and wanting to make amends.

Session 16

There is opportunity for a lengthy discussion of Don's anxieties and fears in connection with the family's trip to the police station to report that one of their bikes had been stolen by a neighbor boy. In the middle of this episode his anxiety has built to the point that he has to go to the bathroom. When he returns, T presses for his feelings at the police station. He at first follows his usual pattern of denial and deflection to someone else; finally he can admit that he did feel nervous and he guesses that is a kind of fear.

Session 17

During early Bobo play, Don pushes his arm down inside Bobo's head and body saying, "Now your mother won't know you." T takes this opportunity to point out that a lot of changes are taking place, but elects not to draw an analogy more directly, at this time, between his quite evident recent movement toward more self-assurance and the possibility that it might be hard for his own mother to accept the change.

Later in this session T attempts to make a comparison between Don's play, of a police alert for an alligator whose friends had trusted him, and his own experience with the neighbor boy. This observation proves to be too abrupt by bringing the fantasy play too quickly back to reality; he pulls away, becomes very quiet, and looks at the clock.

He quickly recovers, as he comments that only five minutes remain, takes a cookie, and laughs, "One for the road." In the final dollhouse scene mother objects to her children sneaking cookies. T again tries the "reality" approach, and is successful this time when she asks if his mother is ever that way with cookies and he admits that she is. As he is leaving he takes a second cookie. T establishes what proves to be a frequent symbol of their rapport as she recognizes and uses his earlier comment, "One for the road."

Session 18

T is a little late getting to the waiting room and finds Don anxiously looking around the corner for her; he denies he was uneasy when T speculates on his feelings.

In this session he takes the lead in transferring playroom events to the real world. As he beats Bobo unmercifully, he exclaims: "Oh, if he were real!" With T's encouragement he talks about wanting to show his friend that he can now stand up for himself—a little, but not enough to destroy the friendship!

When Bobo springs a leak T tries to reassure him that it was not his fault, that other children also play with it, and he just happened to be the one to give the final blow. He volunteers that he knows he couldn't be the only child using the room. T turns this more directly into a discussion of how he feels about her seeing other children. As usual, he denies any jealousy, then distances himself from her all the more by saying he doesn't care who he sees just so long as he sees somebody each time. While engaging in this "put down" of T (because she had been late?), he is tossing a big ball which suddenly comes close to hitting her, much to his obvious surprise.

In retrospect, T's tardiness served as the initial trigger which released, in the playroom, his antagonistic feelings and frustrations with adults as symbols of power. Perhaps, if a child remains too docile and compliant, some tardiness can serve as a useful device to generate meaningful interaction! Children seem to develop more of a common bonding to those with whom they engage in a struggle. At any rate, from this session onward, there were more direct child–therapist interactions; he appeared increasingly to see her as a separate person; and he developed more transference reactions, using T as a substitute mother figure.

His play with the new Slinky toy and the long balloons prompts T to point out his interest today in long things and things that stick out (since the phallic symbolism is quite evident). She also suggests he probably would like to drop the water-filled balloons on the floor to see the splash. He cannot bring himself to let go so daringly, but he does drop them in the sink with evident pleasure. All the events of this session have freed him to the extent that he can spontaneously explain that he is "really mad" as he tries to burst a balloon with darts and knives.

When the hour is up he starts to leave, goes back for a cookie, starts for the door again, and goes back for a second cookie. There is no hesitancy or apparent self-consciousness; rather, he appears to be enjoying his newly discovered capacity for self-indulgence. T's reflection that he seems to need enough supplies to last for the week brings a smiling assent.

Session 19

Having tentatively tested the limits last time by throwing the ball close to T, and being encouraged by T to feel free to mess (with the water balloons), he becomes much more active and daring with the ball, throwing it at the ceiling, then deliberately aiming it at the light. This was the first time T has needed to set a limit, and she is careful to let him know that she knows he really would like to do it.

His two drawings of animals with phallic appendages result in a play disruption when T comments about his extra addition at the rear of the first figure. Perhaps T should have dropped the subject here but instead she makes a comparison with the long bumps hanging from the other figure, at which point he becomes visibly uneasy. In evident reaction to his surprise that his unconscious fantasies are showing through, he immediately plays out a sequence in which a motorcycle cop unthinkingly does all the things he is not supposed to do.

Later, when he blandly gives up his search for darts, T urges him to "face up" to the anger he must be feeling, and he reacts by slapping his own face! T's further urging results in his phoning the police to report the theft of the darts; direct expression of forbidden feelings is still too difficult for him. Nevertheless, he is particularly cheerful as he leaves the session, takes a cookie "for the road" and, for the first time, tells T goodbye.

Session 20

In a further reference to phallic symbols, Don shoots at two round balloons tied on a bottle with two "rat-fink" figures trapped inside. He says the rat-finks are very anxious and don't realize this is all for their own good. Is he expressing his own anxiety about exposing his inner fantasies during the last session? Or is he reflecting some of the probable family discussions of therapy, since father had joined mother in her session last week?

When frustrated at not finding anything suitable for tying off a balloon he gives up with, "Oh well, never mind—but I *do* mind"; quite an admission from this formerly very constricted child. T points out this progress, comparing it to his inability to admit anger directly in the last hour. This is the first session during which he has not kept track of the time; instead he is reluctant to leave even after several reminders from T. He again takes "one for the road."

Session 21

One sequence in this session is particularly meaningful in light of the progress Don has been making and in view of the parental conference two weeks before. A man is rushing to the hospital (the clinic is located in a hospital setting) because he has been told that there has been a change in his son. Father has assumed that the son is getting worse, while actually he is getting better. T keeps her discussion in the third-person frame of reference rather than pointing out comparisons to the real-life situation.

Session 22

Don comes close to testing the limits again as he points the dart gun at T and threatens to shoot on the count of three. It is hard to determine whether he has the impulse to actually shoot at her or whether he now feels free enough to tease and joke with her, in a feeling of camaraderie. In any case T says she guesses he would like to shoot her because she talks too much, that lots of boys feel that way about grown-ups. While he does not comment, neither does he make any denials. Later in the hour, he aims the gun at the clock and talks about shooting it but does not do so.

Session 23

While he is shooting at the baby bottle, T talks about his little brother's use of a bottle when a baby, and asks Don if he ever wanted to imitate him. With his negative comments in this area, she changes direction and suggests he now wants to get rid of babyish ways; this generates considerable boasting about his successful competition with his father and brother in target shooting. When he mentions that Bobo is bleeding, T asks how his nosebleeds are at present. He reports there aren't as many now and he's not as afraid of them as before.

When told that the hour is up, Don demurs saying he has one more thing to do with the darts. He agrees with T's comment that he has recently seemed to not want to leave his sessions. He takes one more shot, starts to leave, returns for his final cookie, and then is ready to go. In effect, he feels he is now ready and able to assume control of his actions and decide for himself when and how he will close a session.

Session 24

The use of a baby bottle as a target is continued in this session and elicit's T's further discussion of his getting rid of baby ways; did people call him a baby or sissy? He responds with, "Yes, but I show them." He then sets up a dart game whereby T must call him a chicken (sissy?) if he misses hitting the bottle. T assumes he expects her to refuse. Instead, she ignores his maneuver to trap her and does go along with his game; he misses and she calls him "chicken." She also points out that his anxiety when he tried so hard had prevented him from succeeding. He agrees with this, calms down, and makes the next shot.

The T–C interactions throughout the remainder of Session 24 are given in such detail in the process notes and theme discussions that further commentary here would be redundant, except to point out the implications of two introductory sequences: (1) with the creation of the Dr. Jekyll juice (made of sand, soap, and red paint), Don, in effect, encourages T to pursue the blood theme throughout; (2) the reference to his "invisible friend" leads to the revelation of his suspicion that the proximity of his mother's therapy room may invade the privacy and security of his playroom. Once reassured on this latter point he proceeds to confess the true identity of his friend (a "she," i.e., mother). Opportunities subsequently unfold for T to elaborate on his suspicions of the quality of the friend's offer of food, and to relate the blood themes from the brew and the paintings to his own nosebleeds and, indirectly, to his mother's hemorrhages.

With respect to the sequence of paintings, T's too intrusive comment about the phallic aspects of the first red painting might well have prevented further pictures. Fortunately, the rapport between T and Don is such, by this point, that he quickly overcomes his anxiety and proceeds, in the second painting, to portray the "invisible friend," and lets T into his deepest secret, that "it is a she" (T has inferred and referred to a boy friend up to this point). He then, with T's help, can express his ambivalence to this bad–good (mother) figure. From here he provides the opening for T to allude indirectly to the bloody experiences he has had with respect to his mother's miscarriages. The inaccessibility of mother is revealed, and explored, in the third painting, as well as references to her poisoning potential. All of this culminates in the final picture of the blind butler, with opportunities for T to point out the castrating aspects of this frightening figure, as well as emphasizing the butler's inability to see (i.e., be with) the girlfriend.

When Don admits that she likes the butler, T stresses Don's probable anger, jealousy, and frustration with this rival for his girlfriend's affection. T's further comments as to whether he would like to get the better of the butler and to keep him away from the girlfriend lead to the vigorous pounding and pummeling of Bobo with its multilayered symbolism.

It would appear that once Don could feel assured that his ambivalent oral wishes and fears have been faced and recognized, and that his babyish dependence on mother has been overcome, he then could proceed to the exploration of his more "mature" oedipal attraction to mother and its attendant competitiveness with father.

At first the parental representations are maintained within the metaphors of "girlfriend" and "butler," but he increasingly enters the fray, culminating in a vigourous personal involvement.

This dramatic transference of the oedipal dilemma into the playroom marks the initiation of observable changes in the tone and character of all subsequent sessions. He will drop all further use of symbolic play figures (puppets, dollhouse dolls, cars, and toy animals). He will interact more directly with the therapist, while transferring both positive and negative maternal roles onto her.

Session 25

Don's initial greeting, to the effect that the time interval since last session seems short, gives T the opportunity to comment on the good session he had last time and how he was able to get a lot of things out. This opening also implies his feeling of a closer bond with T as a result of the previous cathartic session.

Soon he directs T to call him on the toy phone and ask for a cookie, and he actually gives her one, thus confirming his positive feelings with this overt action. (This was his first, and proved to be his only, such offer.) In the remainder of the phone sequence he pulls back from his (inadvertent?) display of affection and generosity by asking exorbitant prices and only pretending to give T the cookies, as he now assumes the role of the begrudging mother. T's reflection of his pretended stinginess, and asking if people ever are that way with him, proves "too close to home" and disrupts the cookie play.

He does continue with the theme of deprivation, but in the context of having T call more distant relatives, until he finally becomes T's young cousin whose mother is stingy with bubble gum. He quickly tries to recover from his own trap by telling T to call back later since he, the cousin, is afraid his mother could listen in. T reassures him that they have a private line (i.e., confirming the privacy of their hour). In assuming the role of T's cousin he also comes close to openly expressing the wish to be

T's son; T's reassurances represent permission for the transference situation to unfold. Thus encouraged, he talks about the mean things he, as cousin, has done to his mother, his frustration at being denied the gum, and his angry reaction of wanting to scream. This is his first emotionalized expression of his anger and frustration with his mother, but he can only experience and verbalize these negative feelings in the context and safety of T's cousin and the cousin's mother.

He comments that the hour has gone too fast and instructs T to make one final call—to her son. In this clear and direct instance of positive transference he makes a frantic plea for her help in saving him from kidnappers (bad parents?), but the more serious and specific danger is a fish (bad mother?) who is eating him up on the spot. T promises to come right away and save him; thus T is cast as a good and rescuing parent who could save him from his unpleasant home situation. He undoubtedly is also expressing his guilt and fear of maternal retaliation for his daring to express the earlier negative feelings toward her.

Session 26

Since Don, by this time, is demonstrating more initiative and positive attitudes as well as being more comfortable in the play situation, T starts the session by asking how things are going at school. His response is far more animated than usual, as he tells her that things are going very, very, very, very well.

During much of the rest of the hour he reverses roles, while using the toy phones, with his being in charge and able to control T. In one sequence he directs T to call her "cousin" but, in an apparent pulling-back from his disclosures in the cousin–son symbols of the previous session, he places obstacles in the way of her making the "connection." Generally, he refuses the requests he instructs her to ask for, while T keeps verbalizing his pattern of obstruction and refusals of help.

Is he reacting to having expressed too much dependence on T, at the end of the previous session, so that he must now undo his casting of her as the good mother? Or are these dramatizations of resistance on his part a reaction to his earlier admission in this session that things were going very well, with the implication that therapy has helped? Since he is forcing her to take the subordinate position and request help, is he making a plea for further help from her by letting her see how it feels to be in need? In any case, he has assumed the role of the parent who is still seen as strict and demanding.

Soon T is again given the part of helper and provider as he, the farmer, asks for quantities of food for his cow, and then for medical care for his dog. He inquires, on the phone, if T is a veterinarian. (One must be sure to have the right kind of doctor—a veterinarian for a dog, but what kind does he himself have? He is to explore this area further in the two following sessions.)

His initial feelings of power are picked up again in his final play with the water pistol in which he is swinging around and shooting randomly, almost shooting T in the process. He does not panic or seem embarrassed, just comments on what almost happened.

Session 27

The last major "blood" reference (and the first since Session 24) occurs early in the session as he makes some bloody looking "tomato juice," with the usual ingredients of sand, soap, and red paint. He assumes the role of feminine provider (Barbara, the cook), masking the underlying evil mother, as he starts to offer the drink to T. His panic when he spills a few drops on the floor is probably doubly determined: horror at the thought that T might actually drink the stuff, and reactivation of his fears of blood. T's discussion of his panic and probable feelings leads him to confess that he sometimes bites his lip so it will bleed to cover up any spills of paint he creates at home. T ties this admission of self-injury to the initial episode of this session when he had stuck a gun up his sleeve, barrel foremost. She goes further and suggests his self-injuries may serve to avoid punishment and to gain sympathy. She further tries to make references to other kinds of blood that might get on the floor at home. His mumbling denials preclude further discussion.

(One may well ask whether T should have more directly discussed his concerns around mother's bleeding and miscarriages. However, T felt that their rapport by this time was such that he knew that she knew and understood what was being displayed symbolically, and that a more direct approach from T might well have elicited too much embarrassment in this still rather restrained child.)

He then shifts to play with the doctor kit. T is the patient and he is the doctor, but a very confused and bumbling one, tapping his own knee for knee jerk and giving shots to himself (again an instance of self-injury). He finally asks T what "species" she is and states that he is a veterinarian. T points out that there are many kinds of doctors and that it is important to go to the right kind. She suggests he is probably wondering what kind of doctors work in the clinic since they don't give shots (one can speculate that there is a deeper concern on his part, if his classmates are asking why he is coming and who he is seeing). He offers to bring in a picture-card of a doctor giving shots to himself as a gift for T.

Session 28

Father accompanies mother again to her session, and T explains to Don that they will be discussing how things are going; and how does he think things are progressing? He is fairly noncommittal but does say he can stand up for himself almost too much now.

He has brought T the promised picture of a doctor, a really horrible looking monster! T takes the opportunity to return to the previous discussions of doctors (Sessions 26 and 27) by suggesting he probably is still wondering what kind of doctors work at the clinic and explains that she is a psychologist. She also pursues her unexpressed feelings of the last session that his friends may be asking questions about his therapy; he admits this was on his mind.

Session 29

As Don describes the frustrating experiences surrounding his birthday celebration he shows very little affect, and then reacts to his inability to shoot the balloons with "failed again." T's reflections on his possible disappointment and anger bring little reaction. When T summarizes that things always seem to go wrong for him, his response is a resigned "That's the way the ball bounces." With subsequent successes at darts he becomes more animated, and T can contrast his earlier feelings with his current glow of success.

Session 30

It is now the middle of May and time to assess progress and to plan for the future. There have been many indications of forward movement: from being overly concerned about cleanliness to acceptance of messes and pleasure at getting things wet; from tight control and inability to accept the freedom of the playroom to free and active use of the materials; from early rationalizations and denials of his fears and inadequacies to spontaneous recognition and expression of feelings; from projection of aggressive urges onto others, to direct physical expressions via Bobo, to the ability to admit and verbalize his own anger. The old ghosts of the bad witch-mother and themes of oral deprivation have all but disappeared; he is ready to meet and match his skills against father and brother; and he seems to have achieved an acceptance of the inevitable outcome of the oedipal struggles. There has been a marked change in his physical appearance from a prissy, immaculately groomed child to one who seems at home in patched jeans and dirty shirts, and he no longer seems to have an inordinate fear of blood.

In view of all of these evidences of improvement T decides to broach the subject of possible termination. It seems unlikely that he or his parents would want to continue in the summer; to consider resumption in the fall, absent any pressing new problems, would undoubtedly undermine the gains achieved to date.

T first asks about home and school and gets a glowing, prideful account of his teacher's call to his mother and how extremely happy everyone is. T suggests that maybe he doesn't need to come anymore if things are going so well. He demurs and says he will have to talk to his mother; T tries to encourage him to make the decision himself in light of what he feels about his therapy, and mother could decide about her therapy. They agree to meet for at least two more sessions, thus giving him time to think about it some more and to talk things over with his mother.

Session 31

Don arrives at the session alone (mother missed her appointment) obviously having decided this would be his last hour. Unfortunately T is a few minutes late; this generates considerable anxiety as he probably fears T has elected, on her own, to terminate even earlier. T reflects his fear and anger at her tardiness and defers until later introducing the question of his decision. When T does bring up the termination issue by asking if he had thought some more about whether he still needs to come, he says he doesn't think he needs to, and bolsters this with a beautiful capsule of his reasons: that he feels he now has "self-confidence." When T suggests that they just meet for the one more agreed-upon date, his hesitation is so apparent that T wonders if he has been feeling he wanted this to be his last session. He is greatly relieved at her recognition and understanding.

The final session often recapitulates the presenting problems, with the child using the toys most frequently used in the past as well as giving some indication of the progress made. Often the final session can be quite a discouraging one for the therapist, in that the child may appear to be regressing, especially if the final session mirrors too closely the initial sesssion in tone and content. It is as if the child is saying, "I hate to leave, I'm afraid to go out on my own, see, I still need help." It may take strong resolve on the therapist's side to resist the urge to retract and decide to resume the sessions; partly because the therapist, also, may be reluctant to terminate the relationship.

Don starts out, on what he has decided was to be his last session, by demonstrating his skill with Bobo, then he moves to the theme of simultaneous oral gratification and deprivation as he assumes the role of food provider. However, he reverts to his initially compulsive approach as he carefully counts and measures spoonfuls of sand onto a pizza pie, in the process using the most anal and messy of the play materials available!

This nurturance is done in the context of appeasing the father figure (the General). In depriving the underdog of anything but the crumbs from the General's table, he may still be resisting, or perhaps finally accepting, his inevitable position of inferiority with respect to father. In assuming the nurturant stance he is also dramatizing the role of mother, who gives most of her affection to father with only a little left for the children.

He then mixes a new concoction in the baby bottle, omitting

the red paint (has that demon been laid to rest?) and retires to the bathroom to work on his secret experiment. Is he still withholding something from T (she immediately suspects masturbatory implications) or is he resolving to keep trying to find solutions? In any event, he is philosophical about his failed experiment, has asserted some independence, and seems on the road to more mature behavior.

Don returns to the phallic balloon and bottle play of recent sessions, announcing that his construction will be enough to last the baby all night. (While the oral–genital symbolism is obvious, in another view this could be interpreted as his feeling that the gains of therapy can be maintained.) When he sticks balloons through his toy spectacles, he remarks on his own changed appearance. (He looks, and feels, like a new person; or he's surprised at the revelation in the displaced phallic imagery.)

As he leaves, he bids farewell to T on an orally gratifying note, smoothing out the messy material into "one last cake" and writing "Goodbye" across the top as a ceremonial decoration.

In retrospect he has, in one way or another, summarized most of the themes from his therapy: resuming his initially compulsive approach to situations; building most of his play and his final farewell gesture out of the messiest of the play materials; capitulating to the father; assuming the role of a good mother who feeds her family; and making several veiled references to the one area which has not been adequately worked through. Only allusions to a totally depriving mother and references to hurts, blood, and injuries are absent from this final session.

From another point of view, each play sequence can be interpreted in either of two ways—in the positive or in the negative—reflecting the basic ambivalence which underlies problem behavior. He plays out deprivation versus gratification, dominance and submission, resistance versus acceptance, dependence versus independence, problems and solutions, and, at last, as frosting on the cake, messiness versus attractiveness.

Finally, he seems to be assessing his own progress when he acknowledges that he has changed and that he now has enough reinforcements to "last all night."

Addendum

Unfortunately, Don's mother misunderstood the clinic's message and, since she had not come to her parallel hour, she insisted that he accompany her to what was originally to have been his final session. T was not expecting him, but could have been called. He valiantly stood by his own decision and did not want her to come.

Two months later, in late summer at a follow-up session, he could openly insist it was his mother's misunderstanding and not his. T, perhaps still feeling guilty for the earlier mix-up in messages, gave him the opportunity to elect to resume therapy in the fall. He responded that he didn't feel he needed to, and T agreed. He left expressing an ambivalent, yet philosophical, outlook toward resuming school in the fall.

Termination Considerations

Several questions can be posed with respect to the termination:

1. Was T justified in her assessment that additional treatment was not essential at this time? Or, should C have been encouraged to continue in view of the fact that at least one theme, masturbatory guilt, had only briefly begun to surface?
2. Should T have let C assume responsibility for deciding that he was ready to terminate?
3. When he announced, during the first of the previously agreed upon two sessions, that this would be his last, should T have left the decision in his hands?

4. There is no information as to why mother missed this crucial session; was she reluctant to agree to her son's decision? Did she feel that if she were not present, then the second session would, of necessity, have to take place?

5. Since his mother missed this session, should she have been called and informed that Don wished to terminate at once? Or would such a call have sent a message to Don that adults were still plotting behind his back, and taking the decision role away from him after all?

6. Should T have made certain to be "on hand" at the hour of the canceled second session, just in case he might appear? Again, what sort of message would have been conveyed?

7. How can one be certain that any therapy process has been adequately completed? Is it enough to launch a child in new directions, with the assurance that therapy can be resumed if or whenever the need may arise again?

Play Disruptions

The phenomenon of "play disruption" was initially described by Erik Erikson (1940) as a sudden break in the child's play, brought on by the play activity suddenly becoming too threatening. Play disruptions may also occur in reaction to a premature or too sudden imposition of a comment or interpretation by the therapist that comes close to uncovering hidden or unconscious impulses. In Don's case, some of the disruptions followed comments by the therapist that drew too obvious a connection to real-life events.

In all instances, play disruptions indicate quite clearly that the current play episode has come close to releasing repressed material. Depending on the child, and the nature of the defenses,

the therapist is faced with the immediate decision as to whether
to call attention to the disruption and then proceed with a
discussion of the theme, or to back off for a little while, mentally
adding this current reaction to previous indicators relating to the
same subject matter. In subsequent sessions, when similar play
themes recur, the therapist can then refer back to the child's
earlier apparent anxieties as a means of aiding the child to
achieve understanding of his or her reactions and underlying
feelings.

Don's first play disruption occurs in the classical Eriksonian
mode. In Session 5 the witch (bad mother figure) has instructed
her two sons to get rid of her worst enemies: another older witch,
dinosaurs, and the policeman. The first two enemies are readily
disposed of, but Don is totally unable to permit the two "son"
figures to eliminate the policeman–father (motorcycle cop), and
the play disintegrates markedly. He finally pulls out by labeling
one of a group of soldiers as the "policeman" after they all are
killed.

In Session 12, a duck and a chicken are riding a horse.
When a toy man asks to join them, the smaller animals object. T
interprets this scene too directly in terms of the "children not
wanting the father around." This obviously proves too threatening a reference to real life and he drops the play. But T has
received confirmation that some negative affects are associated
with father, and this can be used at a later date.

The next two incidents of play disruption (in Sessions 16
and 17) arise in the context of the traumatic episode of a neighbor
child stealing the minibike. While he is reporting on the necessary family visit to the police station, he blocks when trying to
remember the boy's last name. This necessitates a quick trip to
the bathroom—the only recorded instance. In the following
session he becomes silent, and looks at the clock, when T
attempts to relate his play episode of a helpful animal being
wanted by the police to his real life experience of finding out that

his neighbor had also been wanted by the police. Yet later in this session he can readily admit that his dollhouse play (father demanding a clean house, mother not liking her children to sneak cookies) mirrors real events at home. So he gradually begins to accept the concept that play can mirror reality.

In Session 19, T's comment about things hanging down from the two animals he is drawing terminates the drawing activity abruptly, but does provide clues as to what, for him, appear to be unmentionable concerns. This view is confirmed in the succeeding play where the policeman is so upset that he unconsciously breaks all the rules (i.e., does all the prohibited activities).

A few sessions later T's comment about a similar phallic aspect of his first red painting (Session 24) brings about an abrupt shift: he has pointed out one feature saying it looked like a face, then points to an inverted U-shaped curve and say he doesn't know what that could be. When T suggests it looks like a penis, he abruptly turns the sheet over. Luckily he is not deterred, and continues with three still more revealing paintings.

While he is assuming the role of cookie-giver (Session 25), but raising the price each time, T draws an analogy to real life as she suggests maybe people don't freely give him all he wants. He quite suddenly drops that play sequence and shifts to other imaginary phone conversations. Nevertheless, he soon returns to the deprivation theme but now in the context of T's "cousin" whose mother is depriving him of goodies. T's interpretations within this third-person metaphor prove productive and culminate in his assuming the role of T's son who is in danger of being devoured by a fish (the orally aggressive mother).

The final instance of play disruption occurs in Session 27, as a function of his reactions to redness and blood. When he inadvertently spills a few drops of his red "tomato juice" (translate as blood) on the floor, his sudden panic puts an end to the tea party in progress. Since the mixture contained the same ingredients as the "Dr. Jekyll juice" of Session 24, the similarities probable rekindled the whole range of affects elicited in that session, as well as the similar method for disposing of the brew. He then shifts to playing with the doctor kit. He, as doctor, is bumbling and confused, doing all the wrong things and "examining" himself. (Is he trying to work through his embarrassment at spilling the "juice" by hiding it with the clumsy behaviors of others?)

Summary of the Therapeutic Process

The course of therapy has followed a typical pattern in that the initial sessions involved working through the child's defensive shield before any progress could be made toward approaching the affects and impulses being defended against. Once this was accomplished, the earlier pregenital levels of structure were explored before concentrating on oedipal concerns.

In retrospect, it appears that Don's potentially compulsive character was still in the process of formation and had not yet been consolidated into a firmly entrenched position. This made it easier to penetrate his defenses. His patterns of denial, projection, rationalization, reaction formation, and undoing were repeatedly demonstrated and discussed until the underlying affects (fears, angers, disappointments, and guilt) could gradually be highlighted and then openly expressed.

As became apparent, the oedipal complex had not been adequately resolved as the result of too many unsolved problems still lingering from earlier stages. With the lifting of the defenses, the presenting problems in the anal–urethral area could be alleviated, thus making possible the much needed exploration of the earliest deprivations and assaults experienced in the oral period. The very early establishment of the negative maternal image of an orally depriving and orally aggressive mother, one who could neither give nor receive affection, had become closely tied to aspects of mother's perceived potential as a dangerous, castrating figure. Combined with this fear of damage to himself were fears for mother's safety and the haunting guilt that he may somehow have been responsible. This in turn would lead to a magnification of the perceived dangers inherent in any attempted rivalry with father. The compulsive rituals were evidently established as a defense not only against anal–urethral impulses but also against masturbatory desires. All of the above had combined to delay and distort any positive movement into the phallic– oedipal stage because of the further dangers involved. In his unconscious fantasies mother was seen as rejecting his affection, father as too powerful a rival, and he, the child, was left feeling lonely, unloved, and isolated.

After reliving and reworking the conflicts and affects associated with the earlier stages, he then could reenact the oedipal triangle situation whereby he competes in fantasy with father for mother's attention and affection. As a consequence there was a marked change in his demeanor; he demonstrated more instances of positive transference toward the therapist and fairly radiated an aura of self-confidence. As Anna Freud (1965) has pointed out, the adequate resolution of the oedipal conflict yields dividends in insight and self understanding.

Assessing progress from a different point of view, one sees that in the early sessions (1–12) Don has played out his fantasies through the medium of play materials. Cars, animals, soldiers, and puppets were assigned various roles and emotional components in the family and self constellations. For the next six sessions (13–18) he moved from his indirect and symbolic play via the toys to direct attacks on the Bobo figure, setting himself up as a direct combatant in the struggle for power.

From here (in Sessions 19–23) he dared to test the limits of the playroom and achieved the ability to label and express his feelings verbally. Thus "released" he could reenact the oedipal struggle in Session 24. Now he used yet another medium (red paint) to pull together and express the crucial events that had been troubling him—the oedipal longings and jealousies, castration fears, and the multidetermined aspects of blood and bleeding.

Finally, during the last six sessions (25–31), the playroom props seemed scarcely necessary. There was much more direct interaction with the therapist, as well as communicating with her via the toy phones, when he set up different family-based episodes. Positive transference reactions were in evidence; he offered food (some good and some bad) to the therapist; he verbally explored the structure of therapy itself and the doctor–patient relationship; and finally he could state with satisfaction what therapy had done for him.

References

Allen, F. H. (1942), *Psychotherapy with Children*. New York: W. W. Norton.

Axline, V. M. (1947), *Play Therapy*. Boston: Houghton Mifflin.

Cain, A. C., Erikson, M. E., Fast, I., & Vaughan, R. A. (1964), Children's disturbed reactions to their mother's miscarriage. *Psychiat. Med.*, 24:58–66.

Cooper, S., & Wanerman, L. (1977), *Children in Treatment: A Primer for Beginning Psychotherapists*. New York: Brunner/Mazel.

————— —————(1984), *A Casebook of Child Psychotherapy: Strategies and Technique*. New York: Brunner/Mazel.

Coppolillo, H. P. (1987), *Psychodynamic Psychotherapy of Children*. Madison, CT: International Universities Press.

Ekstein, R. (1966), *Children of Time and Space of Action and Impulse*. New York: Appleton-Century-Crofts.

Erikson, E. H. (1940), Studies in the interpretation of play: I. Clinical observation of play disruption in young children. *Genet. Psychol. Monogr.*, 22:557–671.

————(1950), *Childhood and Society*. New York: W. W. Norton, 1963.

————(1959), Identity and the Life Cycle. *Psychological Issues*, Monograph 1. New York: International Universities Press.

Fraiberg, S. H. (1951), Clinical notes on the nature of transference in child analysis. *The Psychoanalytic Study of the Child*, 6:286–306. New York: International Universities Press.

————(1959), *The Magic Years*. New York: Scribner's.

————(1966), Further considerations of the role of transference in latency. *The Psychoanalytic Study of the Child*, 21:213–236. New York: International Universities Press.

Freud, A. (1922–1935), *Introduction to Psychoanalysis. The Writings of Anna Freud*, Vol. 1. New York: International Universities Press, 1974.

————(1936), *The Ego and the Mechanisms of Defense. The Writings of Anna Freud*, Vol. 2. New York: International Universities Press, 1966.

————(1965), *Normality and Pathology in Childhood*. New York: International Universities Press.

Halpern, F. (1953), *A Clinical Approach to Children's Rorschachs*. New York: Grune & Stratton.

Haworth, M. R., & Keller, M. J. (1964), The use of food in therapy. In: *Child Psychotherapy*, ed. M. R. Haworth. New York: Basic Books, pp. 330–338.

Jackson, L., & Todd, K. M. (1947), *Child Treatment and the Therapy of Play*. London: Methuen.

Klein, M., (1932), *The Psycho-Analysis of Children*. London: Hogarth Press.

Klopfer, B., Ainsworth, M. D., Klopfer, W. G., & Holt, R. R. (1954), *Developments in the Rorschach Technique*, Vol. 1. New York: World Book Co.

McDermott, J. F., & Harrison, S. I., eds. (1977), *Psychiatric Treatment of the Child*. New York: Jason Aronson.

Moustakas, C. E. (1953), *Children in Play Therapy*. New York: McGraw-Hill.

Taft, J. (1933), *The Dynamics of Therapy in a Controlled Relationship*. New York: Macmillan.

Suggested Readings

Developmental and Psychosexual Stages

Erikson, E. H. (1950), Eight stages of man. In: *Childhood and Society*, rev. ed. New York: W. W. Norton, 1963, pp. 247–274.

Freud, A. (1965), The assessment of normality in childhood. In: *Normality and Pathology in Childhood*. New York: International Universities Press, pp. 54–92.

Josselyn, I. M. (1978), *Psychosocial Development of Children*, 2nd ed. New York: Family Service Association of America.

Peller, L. E. (1954), Libidinal phases, ego development, and play. *The Psychoanalytic Study of the Child*, 9:178–198. New York: International Universities Press.

The Therapeutic Process

Overview

Carek, D. J. (1972), The strategy of child psychotherapy. In: *Principles of Child Psychotherapy*. Springfield, IL: Charles C Thomas, pp. 103–146.

Feigelson, C. I. (1977), On the essential characteristics of child analysis. *The Psychoanalytic Study of the Child*, 32:353–361. New Haven, CT: Yale University Press.

McDermott, J. F., & Char, W. F. (1984), Stage-related models of psychotherapy with children. *J. Amer. Acad. Child Psychiat.*, 23:537–543.

Maenchen, A. (1970), On the technique of child analysis in relation to stages of development. *The Psychoanalytic Study of the Child*, 25:175–208. New York: International Universities Press.

Williams, M. (1972), Problems of technique during latency. *The Psychoanalytic Study of the Child*, 27:598–617. New Haven, CT: Yale University Press.

Introduction to Therapy

Haworth, M. R., Axline, V. M., Allen, F. H., Moustakas, C. E., Erikson, E. H., & Despert, J. L. (1964), The initial session. In: *Child Psychotherapy*, ed. M. R. Haworth. New York: Basic Books, pp. 91–114.

Therapeutic Alliance

Frankl, L., & Hellman, I. (1962), Symposium on child analysis: II. The ego's participation in the therapeutic alliance. *Internat. J. Psycho-Anal.*, 43:333–337.
Keith, C. R. (1968), The therapeutic alliance in child psychotherapy. *J. Amer. Acad. Child Psychiat.*, 7:31–43.

Defenses and Resistances

Bornstein, B. (1951), On latency. *The Psychoanalytic Study of the Child*, 6:279–285. New York: International Universities Press.
Freud, A. (1936), The ego's defensive operations considered as an object of analysis. In: *The Ego and the Mechanisms of Defense. The Writings of Anna Freud*, Vol. 2. New York: International Universities Press, 1966, pp. 28–41.
Pearson, G. H. J. (1968), Resistances. In: *A Handbook of Child Psychoanalysis*, ed. G. H. J. Pearson. New York: Basic Books, pp. 356–366.

Transference and Countertransference

Berlin, I. N. (1987), Some transference and countertransference issues in the playroom. *J. Amer. Acad. Child & Adol. Psychiat.*, 26:101–107.
Fraiberg, S. (1966), Further considerations of the role of transference in latency. *The Psychoanalytic Study of the Child*, 21:213–236. New York: International Universities Press.
Marcus, I. M. (1980), Countertransference and the psychoanalytic process in children and adults. *The Psychoanalytic Study of the Child*, 35:285–298. New Haven, CT: Yale University Press.

Tyson, R. L., & Tyson, P. (1986), The concept of transference in child psychoanalysis. *J. Amer. Acad. Child Psychiat.*, 25:30–39.

Schowalter, J. E. (1986), Countertransference in work with children: Review of a neglected concept. *J. Amer. Acad. Child Psychiat.*, 25:40–45.

Termination

Coppolillo, H. P. (1987), Termination of treatment. In: *Psychodynamic Psychotherapy of Children*. Madison, CT: International Universities Press, pp. 309–333.

Van Dam, H., Heinicke, C. M., & Shane, M. (1975), On termination in child analysis. *The Psychoanalytic Study of the Child*, 30:443–475. New Haven, CT: Yale University Press.

Symbolic Communication

Fantasies and Metaphors

Bettelheim, B. (1976), *The Uses of Enchantment: The Meaning and Importance of Fairy Tales*. New York: Alfred A. Knopf.

DeSantis, V. P. (1986), Nursery rhymes. *The Psychoanalytic Study of the Child*, 41:601–626. New Haven, CT: Yale University Press.

Fraiberg, S. (1954), Tales of the discovery of the secret treasure. *The Psychoanalytic Study of the Child*, 9:218–241. New York: International Universities Press.

Gillman, R. D. (1987), A child analyzes a dream. *The Psychoanalytic Study of the Child*, 42:263–273. New Haven, CT: Yale University Press.

Gondor, L. H. (1957), Use of fantasy communications in child psychotherapy. *Amer. J. Psychother.*, 11:323–335.

Schwartz, E. K. (1956), A psychoanalytic study of the fairy tale. *Amer. J. Psychother.*, 10:740–762.

Shahly, V. (1987), Eating her words. *The Psychoanalytic Study of the Child*, 42:403–421. New Haven, CT: Yale University Press.

Drawings

DiLeo, J. H. (1983), *Interpreting Children's Drawings*. New York: Brunner/ Mazel.

Klepsch, M., & Logie, L. (1982), *Children Draw and Tell*. New York: Brunner/Mazel.

Winnicott, D. W. (1971), Case I 'Irio' *aet* 9 years 9 months. In: *Therapeutic Consultations in Child Psychiatry*. New York: Basic Books, pp. 12–27.

Objects and Activities

Bettleheim, B. (1987), The importance of play. *Atlantic Monthly*, March: 35–46.

Haworth, M. R., & Keller, M. J. (1962), The use of food in the diagnosis and therapy of emotionally disturbed children. *J. Amer. Acad. Child Psychiat.*, 1:548–563.

———— ————(1964), The use of food in therapy. In: *Child Psychotherapy*, ed. M. R. Haworth. New York: Basic Books, pp. 330–338.

Levin, S., & Wermer, H. (1966), The significance of giving gifts to children in therapy. *J. Amer. Acad. Child Psychiat.*, 5:630–652.

Loomis, E. A., Jr. (1957), The use of checkers in handling certain resistances in child therapy and child analysis. *Amer. J. Psychoanal. Assn.*, 5:130–135.

Meeks, J. (1970), Children who cheat at games. *J. Amer. Acad. Child Psychiat.*, 9:157–174.

Schowalter, J. E. (1983), The use and abuse of pets. *J. Amer. Acad. Child Psychiat.*, 22:68–72.

Woltmann, A. G. (1951), The use of puppetry as a projective method in therapy. In: *An Introduction to Projective Techniques*, ed. H. H. & G. L. Anderson. New York: Prentice-Hall, pp. 606–638.

Correlates of Therapy

Amster, F. (1943), Differential uses of play in treatment of young children. *Amer. J. Orthopsychiat.*, 13:62–68.

Anthony, E. J. (1977), Nonverbal and verbal systems of communication. *The Psychoanalytic Study of the Child*, 32:307–325. New Haven, CT: Yale University Press.

Beres, D. (1952), Clinical notes on aggression in children. *The Psychoanalytic Study of the Child*, 7:241–263. New York: International Universities Press.

Bornstein, B. (1953), Masturbation in the latency period. *The Psychoanalytic Study of the Child*, 8:65–78. New York: International Universities Press.

Kaplan, E. B. (1976), Manifestations of aggression in latency and preadolescent girls. *The Psychoanalytic Study of the Child*, 31:63–78. New Haven, CT: Yale University Press.

Maenchen, A. (1984), The handling of overt aggression in child analysis. *The Psychoanalytic Study of the Child*, 39:393–405. New Haven, CT: Yale University Press.

Mittleman, B. (1957), Motility in the therapy of children. *The Psychoanalytic Study of the Child*, 12:284–319. New York: International Universities Press.

Tyson, P. (1980), The gender of the analyst: In relation to transference and countertransference manifestations in prelatency children. *The Psychoanalytic Study of the Child*, 35:321–338. New Haven, CT: Yale University Press.

Weiss, S. (1964), Parameters in child analysis. *J. Amer. Psychoanal. Assn.*, 12:587–599.

Index to Sessions